SAM HILDEBRAND GUERILLA

Other Books by the Author:

The Complete and Authentic Life of Jesse James
The Day Jesse James was Killed
Escapades of Frank and Jesse James
Great Gunfighters of the West
Great Lawmen of the West
Outlaws of the Old West
Date With Destiny: Billy the Kid
Killer Legions of Quantrill
Younger Brothers
The Man Who Shot Jesse James
Forty Years on the Wild Frontier
Quantrill and his Civil War Guerillas
Rube Burrow, King of the Train Robbers
Gunslingers

SAM HILDEBRAND
GUERILLA

by

Carl W. Breihan

Published by
Leather Stocking Books

Pine Mountain Press, Inc., Publishing Group

P.O. Box 13604
Wauwatosa, WI 53226

CREDITS:

Editor: *Judith Harway*

Cover: *E. Lisle Reedstrom*

Typesetting: *Trade Press Typographers*

Manufacturing: ARCATA

Manufactured in U.S.A.

ISBN: 0-89769-076-1

INTRODUCTION

My father, James T. McArtor, rode with Sam Hildebrand a number of times, so I feel that I am qualified to write this brief introduction to Mr. Breihan's history of Sam. My father told me of a fight between the guerrillas and some Federals at a cave on the Missouri River bluffs north of Independence, Missouri. I have heard these stories so many times they are fixed in my mind in spite of my age.

A small body of Quantrill's men under Sam Hildebrand, of which group my father was one, was out on a forage for food and encountered a small party of Federal soldiers, also apparently on a forage. As these men were returning to Independence, Hildebrand and his group cut them off and chased them to the Missouri River bluffs. There they took refuge in a cave. Hildebrand then stationed his men at various positions on the top of the cave and commanded all to be silent. It was like a cat watching a mouse. When a Federal stuck his head out too far to see if the coast was clear one of Hildebrand's sharpshooters picked him off; when others of his group rushed to carry him back into the cave, they too were shot down by a deadly volley from Sam's men. Soon after that Sam withdrew his men back to Quantrill's headquarters.

My father also told about two brothers named Von de Velt of Harrisonville, Missouri. During the border war days they had been stealing slaves, taking them to Kansas, and setting them free after making an arrangement with the slave owner (who did not know they were the thieves) to go to Kansas and return the slaves for a price. Sam Hildebrand was coming from Jackson County, Missouri, with a body of horsemen, my father among them, and they met the Von de Velts returning from Kansas. Hildebrand asked them some questions and from their friendly talk learned of their business. The brothers were promptly covered with pistols and disarmed. They then were led to a trestle of the old Kansas

City, Fort Scott and Memphis Railway, now a system of the Frisco Railroad, and hanged from the ties. Many years later I learned that these two brothers were uncles of my mother-in-law. Such is war!

Once my father, James T. McArtor, was returning from Kansas City to Quantrill's camp on foot, with Sam Hildebrand and several other guerrillas. South of the Blue River, where Sheffield now is, they met a large body of Federal soldiers. This area was about a quarter of a mile from a dry ditch about as deep as a man is tall. The guerrillas ran through the brush, chased by the Federals, each firing at the other as the opportunity presented itself. The men of Hildebrand's group took refuge in this ditch, facing the pursuing soldiers. With cocked muskets ready they waited, but no one appeared. My father put his hat on the end of his ramrod and raised it above the ditch level. Several shots rang out, then silence. The guerrillas grew weary of this, and finally one of them stood up; it turned out that the soldiers had left the area, so Hildebrand and his small group returned to their camp.

Prior to the Battle at Pilot Knob, Missouri, my father, along with some of Hildebrand's men and Sam himself, had come from Arkansas with General Sterling Price and twelve thousand men. The guerrillas did the scout and advance lookout work. Price intended to attack St. Louis, but when he got to Fredricktown he began to change his mind. General Marmaduke had informed him that Union General Rosecrans was bringing up a large body of reinforcements on transport vessels on the Mississippi River. He had other problems too, since his men had to live off the land. This was an easy task for Sam Hildebrand and his small group for they were used to such tactics.

At Farmington, General Price ordered Jo Shelby to tear up the tracks of the Iron Mountain Railroad at Ironton so that Pilot Knob would be cut off from St. Louis. Then he was supposed to overrun Potosi and wait for Price there. At the same time, Marmaduke and Fagan were to overrun a small Union garrison at Fort Davidson near the base of Pilot Knob. This would clear the path for a march to St. Louis.

General Rosecrans had ordered General Ewing at Fort Davidson to hold his ground unless attacked by Price's main army, in which case he was to withdraw to St. Louis. General Ewing was unaware that Price's main force was in the Arcadia Valley until September 26, when their many campfires were sighted.

At Ironton General Price ordered his engineering officer,

Captain T. J. Mackey, to look at the fort from atop Pilot Knob. Mackey advised Price to emplace cannon on Shepherd's Mountain, less than half a mile from Fort Davidson. Such an artillery bombardment would make Fort Davidson an untenable position to hold, but General Price was impatient and thought his troops and the guerrillas could overrun the fort. He launched an attack on Tuesday afternoon, September 27, 1864, across a mile of open flat land. In less than half an hour, General Price had lost a thousand of his best assault troops.

That night, General Ewing and his thousand men slipped out of Fort Davidson and marched north toward Potosi. Price was so angry at being outwitted by General Ewing that he sent Marmaduke and Shelby in hot pursuit, but the Federals fought such a successful rear-guard action that Ewing and his men were able to escape.

This is the story of Pilot Knob as told to me by my father, who participated in the fray with Sam Hildebrand and company. These facts were also carried in the many notes that my father left, which were given to Mr. Breihan for his use.

Reading this manuscript about Sam brings back many things that I was told by my father and others concerning Sam's part during the war in Missouri. I know of no such other work devoted to the life and times of Sam Hildebrand, and I am glad to see such a work available to the people. Mr. Breihan has done an excellent job in telling this story as he always does.

Edward McArtor
Lakeland, Florida

Author's note: *Many of the incidents mentioned herein have been attested to by Sam's nephew, L. J. Hildebrand.*

CHAPTER 1

Samuel S. Hildebrand was born on January 6, 1836, the fifth of the ten children of George and Rebecca Hildebrand. He was proud of his ancestry and frequently claimed that his progenitors had been important in the history of Germany, belonging to the group of people that originated the Dutch language. After being driven out of Bavaria during the wars of the sixteenth century, they were among the earliest settlers in Pennsylvania. They pressed on toward the west, always resisting city life, preferring the hardships of the forest while they helped beat the Indians further and further into the wilderness.

As stated at that time, "they continually breathed the pure air and trod through the dewy vales and drank at Freedom's shady fountains among the unclaimed hills."

After the death of Samuel's grandfather, who had lived to be a century old, George and Rebecca moved their family further into the wilderness. They settled along one of the tributaries of the Meramec River, which emptied into the Mississippi River about twenty miles south of St. Louis. During the years when they were raising their ten children they built a two-story stone house along the fertile bottom lands of Big River in St. Francois County, west of the Mississippi. They had to fell the timber in order to prepare farmland, and after a few years they owned barns, cribs, and stables. The Indians in this section were periodically hostile, however, and one day a delegation from the Lt. Governor of Louisiana arrived to advise them to leave the area because of frequent Indian depredations.

The Hildebrands moved to Ste. Genevieve. Sam said later, "The Federal government's extensive military operations in southwest Missouri were in great measure designed for my special destruction."

While Sam was growing up there was no custom among his acquaintances to do anything but hunting and fishing or exploring along the majestic bluffs that walled the sides of the crooked and romantic Big River. He later recalled that he had actually attended school one day — one day was enough to give him a distaste for the very sight of a schoolhouse.

As he later said, "I only learned the name of two letters, one shaped like the gable end of a roof and the other shaped like an ox yoke standing on end. At recess time the boys got to picking on me, and I had every one of them to whip. When the teacher came out and started talking saucy, I gave him a good cursing and ran home. My father said I either had to go to school or work on the farm, and I gladly accepted the work. Always afterward I took pains to please my father. A threat to send me to school was all the whipping I ever needed."

After his father's death in 1850 Sam continued to support his mother and the rest of the family by staying and working on the homestead. But after his nineteenth birthday he married Margaret Hampton on October 30, 1854. He was proud to join her family, and he built a neat log house, setting up a farm of his own within a mile of his family. There was always an abundance of stock, especially hogs. The uplands constituted an endless forest of oaks, so there was a plentiful supply of acorns, food for the hogs that roamed the woods and became quite numerous. Whenever they showed enough fat for pork, Sam killed many of them with his gun and dogs, and that added to the prosperity of the year.

A colony of Pennsylvania Dutch established themselves in the neighborhood, and they soon constituted two-thirds of the population of the township. Claiming that they too owned hogs, they set up "wild hog claims". They brought up many little lawsuits before the Justice of the Peace, declaring that some of their own hogs ran wild. The Hildebrand family was branded as "hog thieves," because they fought to hold control of the woods.

As new neighbors arrived they, in turn, became prejudiced against the Hildebrands. It was said that the Hildebrands "loved pork a little too well and needed watching." The majority of the neighbors were in favor of the Union, as Sam was too, but unfortunately they did not turn out to be friendly. Sam knew there were rumors of a possible war, but he had no opinion of the causes. He did know that his neighbors and enemies were making preparations to leave their families as comfortable as possible in case they had to take up arms for their country. There were also some in sympathy with the South, many of whom had no visible means of earning a livelihood, not even a horse to ride. In fact, the value of every horse at such a time only encouraged horse stealing.

Sam said, "Horse stealing was not confined to either party, and it was remarkable how political sentiments of a horse-pressing renegade differed from the neighbor who happened to have the fastest horses."

CHAPTER 2

When the Great Rebellion started in the spring of 1861, Sam called on some good citizens who were not Republicans. Knowing that they were better posted than he was on the current events, he asked them what was best for him to do. Their advice was, "Stay at home and attend to your own business." So he put in a crop of corn at the usual season and cultivated it during the summer, paying no attention to what was going on throughout the county.

On the 9th day of August excitement spread throughout the county because of the killing of a Union man, Mr. Ringer. He was shot at his own house by Allen Roan and Tom Cooper, men who did not agree with his political ideas. Sam felt the impact of this event because Allen Roan was a relative of his with whom he was on friendly terms. Naturally, those neighbors who already had a grudge against him for other reasons now suspected him, and what they called the "Hildebrand gang" was blamed for the murder.

Sam was advised by a Union friend not to take any part in the matter, for anything he might do would only bring disaster upon himself. He had every intention of obeying this advice but, as he said later, "I was caught in a cunningly devised trap that settled my destiny forever."

One evening Allen Roan came to Sam's field where he was

plowing and suggested swapping horses. Sam looked over the horse he was offering and concluded that the exchange would be a good business. However, he quickly discovered that the new horse would not work in harness, so the very next day he swapped him for one owned by a Mr. Rogers.

Shortly before this some of Sam's neighbors had started what they called a Vigilante Committee, and their squads patrolled night and day to put down horse stealing. At the head of that gang was Firman McIlvaine, the worst element in the community. Along with James Craig, John House, Joe McGahan, John Dunwoody, William Patton and others, he swore death to any man implicated with the southern recruits, especially if they were pressing horses.

The horse which Allen Roan had left with Sam, and which Sam had turned over to Rogers, proved to be the property of Dunwoody. A friend came around at night and warned Sam that he and his brother Frank were both threatened with death if they could be found. Although they were both innocent in this matter, there was nothing for them to do but hide out. As Sam said at the time, "When the law is wrested from the civil authorities by such men, anything like a trial would not be permitted."

Sam and Frank secreted themselves in the woods, hoping that matters would take a different turn in a short time. Sam would willingly have surrendered to the civil authorities with a guarantee of a fair trial, but in face of the threat of an unscrupulous mob he had no alternative but to hide. The search continued for Frank and Sam throughout October, and they suffered even more for blankets than for food. After three weeks Sam decided to risk getting to see his family in order to get some food to eat and bed clothes.

It was about eleven o'clock at night when he got within sight of his house. There was no light showing, and he heard no noise of any kind. He whispered "Margaret" through a crack in the wall, and his wife noiselessly opened the door to let him in. They talked in whispers, and she placed some supper on the table. Just when he was about to start eating he heard the top rail fall off his yard fence.

Immediately he took up his gun in one hand, a loaf of corn bread in the other, and stepped into the yard by the back door. McIlvaine and his vigilantes had come into the yard and were approaching the house from all sides in a regular line. Sam detected a gap in their ranks and dashed through it. They commenced firing, and Sam dodged behind a molasses mill in the yard. That mill caught nine of their bullets and, without doubt, saved Sam's life. Then he struck out towards the woods, a distance of about 200 yards. He had the inclination to shoot back at them, but that would indicate where he was in the open field, so he silently gained the edge of the woods. From there he could hear the men talking and thus became certain of his enemies' identity.

Sam felt grateful that he had escaped. He gnawed at the bread loaf, trying to reconcile himself to the state of affairs. He was certain now that he would not be allowed to remain in the vicinity of his home. There was nothing for him to do but set out without a dollar in his pocket, deserting his beloved family. Neither he nor Frank had anything except one horse and the clothing on their backs.

After the mob had apparently left, Sam's wife walked out of the house and found him in the woods. Together they made plans. She returned home and dressed their five children, and quietly brought them out to the woods at a spot he had designated. Then she returned and saddled Sam's horse, packing him with bed clothes and provisions. She rode his horse through the hills and joined Sam at an appointed place five miles away from their beloved home.

There they remained until night returned, at which time they proceeded together, avoiding the mud and occasional pools of water. Sam carried his gun on his shoulder and one of the children on his hip. His wife packed the baby in her arms and walked silently by his side. Sam said afterward, "I never before was so deeply impressed with the faith, energy, and confiding spirit of a woman."

When daylight appeared they were at Wolf Creek, a few miles south of Farmington. There they stopped in the woods to cook a breakfast and rest a while. During the day they proceeded to Flat Woods, eight miles from Farmington, in the southern part of St. François County, about ten miles north of Fredericktown. Sam contacted his friend Mr. Griffin, and in a very short time they had the use of a log cabin in a remote locality. The Hildebrands were installed in a new home.

CHAPTER 3

When Sam and his family managed to get out of the woods, it must have troubled them considerably that Frank had chosen to remain a while longer so as not to disrupt his home and family any more than necessary. As a matter of fact, he remained shivering in the woods until the middle of November when he could endure the cold no longer. Accepting the advice of his friend Franklin Murphy he made his way to Potosi, where he applied to Captain Castleman and offered to join the Home Guards.

Although it had not occurred to him, Castleman was intimate with Firman McIlvaine, and he detained Frank until he had sent word to McIlvaine. In this way he betrayed Frank into the hands of the mob that was looking for him.

At first, McIlvaine made a gesture to keep the arrest within the law, escorting Frank to the Justice of the Peace on Big River. Frank was willing to be tried because he knew he was innocent; however, Franklin Murphy, the Justice of the Peace, insisted he had no authority except to commit Frank to jail until he could be tried in the proper court. Naturally McIlvaine was not willing to allow Frank to have this reprieve. Hoping to demonstrate that the charge was beyond Murphy's jurisdiction, they now claimed that Frank had stolen a horse in Ste. Genevieve County. Thereupon the mob took Frank to Punjaub, in Ste.

Genevieve County, before Justice R. M. Cole.

When Justice Cole said, "I am a sworn officer of the law, and therefore I require evidence against this prisoner. Without that I can only commit him to jail until proper trial can be held," McIlvaine and his buddies made up an entirely different story.

"But this man has stolen a mule in Jefferson County," they said. "In fact, he went with Sam Anderson late at night to the home of a Mr. Carney to steal his mare. Mrs. Carney heard them at the gate and went out to tell them that her husband was not at home, for he had ridden the mare to a neighboring town. Then," they further claimed, "Frank forced Mrs. Carney to go with him a quarter of a mile in her night clothes to show them where Mr. Becket lived. Finally they went there and stole his horse."

Justice Cole was not convinced by this argument, so the mob left his court with their prisoner, insisting that they were going to take him to Jefferson County for trial.

They took Frank about five miles out of town and hung him in the forest without any kind of trial at all. Then they flung his body into a sink-hole thirty feet deep. It was more than a month before his body was found.

A few weeks later, Firman McIlvaine boasted that Frank had been hung by his express orders. He said the murder had taken place on November 20, 1861, about one month after Frank's brother Sam escaped with his family.

A short time after Sam and his family arrived in Flat Woods, he made his way back to his former home, hoping to rescue some of his property. Arriving at the silent house he discovered that everything had been removed. A friend reported that the Vigilante Committee had wantonly destroyed everything they did not want for their own use. Sam returned to Flat Woods to rejoin his family in a very despondent mood, to say the least.

The Union men were all joined against him, although Sam still wanted to avoid taking part in the national struggle. He told someone that he considered the war "a rich man's war and a poor man's fight." Still, he felt deeply wronged, reduced to absolute poverty, and mourned the loss of his brother. It seemed all the fault of the rich man Firman McIlvaine. As the battles raged, Sam remained with his family, doing all he could to provide for them, and always alert in case any of his enemies should locate his present whereabouts.

The Vililante Committee activities culminated in the formation of a company of militia on Big River, with James Craig for captain and Joe McGahan first lieutenant. They were now in a position to disarm southern sympathizers and seize the contraband of war, such as arms and ammunition. Their cry of "disloyal" could be raised against any man who happened to have property. In their terms, "arms" could mean *armchairs,* or anything else they could get their hands on. "Guns" included *Gunn's Domestic Medicine.* A fine claybank mare was confiscated because she looked *fiery.* And a spotted mule was confiscated because it had so many *colors.* They took a gun from Mr. Metts merely because he lived on the *south side* of Big River. They destroyed some of the estate of Dick Poston by killing the cattle for beef and dividing it among themselves under the pretext that if Dick Poston had been living he most undoubtedly would have been a Rebel.

In the meantime, Sam's house at Flat Woods was far from safe. Sam and his family spent six months of tranquility there by the time the members of the Vilante Committee learned of their whereabouts in April, 1862. Firman McIlvaine collected eighty soldiers from Ironton to aid in Sam's capture.

One day Sam was hauling wood, and when he unloaded the wagon he stepped into the house. Suddenly he spotted the eighty vigilantes, within gunshot and coming under full charge. Sam seized his gun and dashed through a gap in their lines ("that Heaven had left open for my escape," he explained later). While they were firing at him, he ran through some thick brush and jumped over a picket fence. Out of the hundreds of bullets sent after him, one struck his leg below the knee and broke a bone. He clutched the bushes, holding up as well as possible. They had to stop to throw down the fence, and during that time he scrambled along about two hundred yards farther. Crouching in a gully that was half full of leaves, he was able to bury himself completely from sight. He could hear the soldiers rushing around, scouring the woods in every direction. Finally they returned to burn down the house and all Sam's possessions. Then they left, perhaps satisfied.

One possible reason the Federal soldiers did not remain in the area longer was that sixteen of Captain Bolin's men representing the South had been seen crossing the gravel road the day before. Captain Bolin was a Rebel officer with headquarters in Greene County, Arkansas. Under his command some daring spirits had been led on to deeds of heroism.

Now Sam's condition was truly deplorable. As he lay in the gully, covered with leaves and with one leg rendered useless, he realized that once again his family was without shelter. All of their possessions had been burned. As he lay there, suffering the wounds inflicted by U.S. soldiers, he declared a war of his own. He swore that he would destroy as many of them as he could. He even said, "To submit to further insult would be an insult to the Being who gave me the power of resistance."

Sam's wife came in search of him when it seemed that he enemies had left. Sam told her to come after dark to dress his leg if she could be sure that nobody was watching. Fortunately, she was able to find Mr. Pigg, and she brought him back to Sam. He did everything in his power to relieve Sam's suffering, even supplying the family with bedding and provisions. After dark he removed them all to a place of safety. While Sam nursed his wound, his place of concealment was known only by the few men who could be trusted.

There were many hours of loneliness now during which Sam could reflect upon his situation. He demanded silently, "What have I done to merit a persecution so cruel?" He half resolved to go to some other state in order to avoid the war. But Southern men, the only men with whom he could talk about his difficulty, assured him that this only safety would be flight to the army of the South. The Vigilante Committee had destroyed every vestige of good feeling he had formerly felt for the Union people. He was now on record with both civil and military authorities as a horse thief — and a very dangerous man. It seemed that there was no chance of his ever regaining his former status, to enjoy life as a private citizen.

Sam secretly declared himself a Rebel. While his wife doctored his wounded leg, his friend sent word to one of Captain Bolin's men to come to his relief. A man was dispatched to learn the particulars of the case. Sam answered many questions but was told nothing. The next night he was lifted into a light spring wagon among boxes of drugs and medicines. He was told that his wife and children would be taken to Captain Bolin and protected until they could rejoin him. A guard of two men watched over him the whole night without speaking one word. The route led through woods, and Sam was tumbled about rather roughly among the boxes.

At daylight the wagon stopped in desolate country. They had traveled along the western side of the St. Francis River and were now camped near its most western bend, near the southern line of Madison County. As they remained there all that day, Sam was able to indulge in short naps. It was only after dark that the journey continued, bearing to the eastward. The road was so rough that Sam was glad when, about eight o'clock the next morning, the wagon was halted on the western bank of the St. François River, midway between Bloomfield in Stoddard County and Crane Creek in Butler County.

A scouting party from General Jeff Thompson's camp came riding up, crying, "Well, boys! What have you in your wagon?"

"Drugs and medicines from Captain Bolin's camp."

On hearing this they dismounted and kept up a lively conversation around the campfire. Among their number was a jovial fellow who kept the rest all laughing. Sam, lying in the wagon, thought he recognized that voice. He turned over to peep through a hole in the wagon bed, and the man he was trying to look at heard the strain of the wagon at Sam's weight.

"Who in thunderation have you got in the wagon?" he demanded.

"Some fellow from St. Francois county, wounded and driven off by the Federals."

"The devil! Why, that is my native country. I'll take a look at the fellow. It's Sam Hildebrand, as I live! How do you do, old rapscallion?"

"Well, well! If I haven't run across Tom Haile, the daredevil of the swamps!"

"Old drugs and medicine, eh? What are you doing here? Trying to pass yourself off as a great medicinal root, I suppose. Say, Sam, did you bring some good horses down with you?"

"Hush, Tom! If they find out I'm not a horse thief they'll drum me out of camp."

The party prepared to start again. The first man who attempted to mount nearly dashed to the ground in consequence of the rattling of a tin cup that someone had tied to his spur.

Tom said, "It's a perfect shame to treat any man in that way."

The man in question seemed to think so too, judging from the glance he cast at Tom. But they mounted, set off through a muddy puddle and over a rocky point, and soon they were far away in the hills.

Sam's contraption started up again and traveled until about midnight. They paused at the State line between Missouri and Arkansas and remained there until morning. Soon they were riding through Greene County, Arkansas, and during the day they arrived safely at the headquarters of Captain Bolin. Sam was received into the group of families there for mutual protection, most of them the families of Captain Bolin's men.

Sam's wound by this time was doing well, and he felt for a time quite at home.

CHAPTER 4

As soon as Sam was able to ride, he got the use of a horse and went hunting for Captain Bolin in order to make a real connection with the Rebel army. Several other men went along with him, across the swampy country east of the St. Francis River. He was not at all sure what dangers he might encounter, so he was relieved to reach the headquarters of General Jeff Thompson in safety. While waiting for an appointment he sauntered about the camp, now and then meeting acquaintances from Missouri and actually getting news from home.

At last he was admitted to General Thompson's quarters and was received cordially. The General listened with sympathy while Sam described his recent ordeals — how his brother had been murdered and how he himself had narrowly escaped a similar fate.

Seizing a pen, General Thompson rapidly wrote a few lines and handed Sam the paper, saying, "Here! I'm giving you a major's commission. Go where you please, take along any men you can pick up. Fight on your own hook, and report to me every six months."

Sam crammed the paper into his pantaloon pocket and walked out with the first feeling of satisfaction he had known for a long time. He knew he could not read his commission, but at the same time he was determined not to ask anyone else to read it for him. He had to protect his new honor.

Sam went off a little distance off from the camp and seated himself on an old cypress log. He had to take time to reflect on what the name "Major Sam Hildebrand" would look like in the history books of the future. Of course he was not entirely comfortable in this unexpected position because he knew nothing about military tactics. He was not even certain whether a major held sway over a general or whether he was merely a bottlewasher under some captain. He decided that, if the latter was the case, he would return to Greene County and serve under Captain Bolin.

The biggest problem at the moment was how to get enough money to buy shoulder straps to show his rank. Of course, he could always fight without them. For several days he remained in camp, trying to catch on to whatever he might do to help the Rebels in their fight, mysterious though that fight seemed to be. He listened to tales of blood and pillage from scouts who came in from various directions.

At any rate, his wound was practically healed and, mounting a horse that was provided for the new major, he made his way back to Greene County, arriving at Captain Bolin's headquarters feeling like his old self.

Captain Bolin said, "I;ve been hearing about you from one of my scouts, and I'm glad you've gotten here. I presume you've already been to General Thompson's camp. Did you see the 'Old Swamp Fox'?"

"I did."

"What did he do for you?"

Sam pulled his commission out of his pocket. By now it looked like a piece of gunwadding. Captain Bolin gave it a glance and then looked Sam over from head to toe.

"Well, Major Hildebrand — " he began.

"Sam, if you please."

"Very well, Sam. What do you propose to do?"

"Well, Captain, the General formed me into an independent company of my own — told me to pick up a few men and do what I can. When I go against my old personal enemies up in Missouri I guess I'm expected to do a *major* part of the fighting myself."

At this the Captain laughed heartily. After rummaging in an old box, he drew forth something that looked like a bottle; it was not necessary for Sam to ask what that was for. Actually, they made a little ceremony of it.

Then Captain Bolin said, "Well, sir, the commission I obtained is of the same kind. I now have 125 men, and we are what is known as 'Bushwhackers.' We carry on a war against our enemies by shooting them. My men are from various sections of the country, and each one has some grievance to redress at home. In order to give each man a chance to do his best, we give him all the help he may require. After he sets things right in his part of the country, he comes back and helps others with their own problems. We thus swap work as the farmers do in harvest time. If you want to unite your destiny with ours, you will be entitled to all our privileges."

Captain Bolin's proposition pleased Sam immensely. He knew little and cared less about the merits of the war, but he was delighted to belong to a large army, and he was even pleased to be under strict discipline. He would not have been satisfied to stand up in a column numbering thousands of men. He didn't even want to be hurled in regular order against a mass of men covering three or four miles square and against whom he had no personal spite. That would never have satisfied his spirit of revenge.

Sam thought, "Even in a fierce battle between two opposing armies, not more than one man out of ten can succeed in killing his man. In a battle of that kind he would have no more weight than a gnat in a bull's horn." He was delighted to be in the "Bushwhacking Department," with the continent for a battlefield and the woods for his headquarters.

Eager to get started, his wound still made it necessary to hang around camp for another six weeks. Unfortunately, as long as he stayed in Arkansas he could not hear any news of his family because the Federals controlled every town in that section of the country including of course, all the roads between counties.

On the first of June, 1862, Sam was furnished a horse and, with his faithful gun that he called "Kill-Devil", he set out on his first trip back to Missouri. Knowing that the success of his project depended on the secrecy of his movements, he was glad to go alone. He managed to do all his traveling at night, and even then usually within the woods. From Captain Bolin's men he had learned the names and whereabouts of Southern sympathizers along the route, so he traveled slowly to favor his wound as well as to make new friends.

When Sam arrived in the vicinity of Flat Woods in St. François County, Missouri, it was the 12th day of June. Immediately, he commenced searching for George Cornecious, the man who had reported his whereabouts to McIlvaine and the soldiers. It was Cornecious who had caused him to be wounded and driven out of Flat Woods. After searching for two days and nights he succeeded in connecting with that traitor, and there was real satisfaction for Sam shooting him to death while managing to remain in hiding.

That was the beginning of his careful campaign to rid the world of all his enemies. He used his time to good advantage, and by June 23rd he spent the daylight sleeping under an overhanging rock beside the river on the fish dam. Stealthily he crossed the river and went to the lower part of McIlvaine's farm. There he found Negroes cutting down a field of rye. They worked steadily for several hours, until they had it down within one hundred yards of the fence.

Sam had been waiting, well hidden. At last he saw McIlvaine making his first round. Actually, he passed where Sam was hiding and he stopped to whet his scythe. As soon as he had done that, he lowered the cradle to the ground and stood resting against the handle.

Sam fired, and McIlvaine was dead. Nothing but a long series of wrongs could have made him take the life of a young man who had so many good points. Sam remembered how, after the first outbreak of war, a fine mare had been stolen from McIlvaine. He must have loved that mare, and when others told him that Sam Hildebrand was the thief, he must have felt a righteous anger. And so he was goaded on to take the law into his own hands. Because of all that, Frank Hildebrand had been hung without a trial and his body flung into a sink-hole to moulder like that of a beast. Sam suffered all over again at the memory of this crime against the brother he loved. Then more memories assailed him: his loving wife and family had been forced to pass through hardships they did not deserve. Sam saw again the tearful eyes of the children he loved and the pale face of his wife who stood by him so faithfully.

Sam's revenge had been long delayed, but now it had come he did not relish it because in his heart he knew it was not fair to McIlvaine, no matter how much damage he had caused because of the loss of his mare. Sam knew the real cause of so much misery was the man who stole that mare.

Although this became clear while he observed McIlvaine's sudden death, he still could not delay wreaking the rest of his revenge. He could not return to Arkansas before finishing off Joe McGahan and John House, who had both been very officious in the Vigilante mob. He posted himself in the woods within a hundred yards of McGahan's house at daylight. He remained there watching all day, but McGahan did not appear until dark began to creep over the landscape. Then he rode up and immediately went into his house. It was now too dark for Sam to shoot at such a distance, so he moved to the garden fence. Within a few minutes McGahan appeared at the door of his house with a little child in his arms. The fence prevented Sam from shooting McGahan below the child in his arms, and if he shot toward his breast he would kill the child. He had to hold his hatred.

McGahan remained standing in the doorway a minute or two, and then he returned into the house. Sam was so emotional at the moment that he was not prepared to shoot when McGahan suddenly left the house and rode off. Sam went back to the thicket and slept until it was nearly day. Then he took his position near the house again, and he watched until night again set in. Sam later said, "Fortunately for him he did not make his appearance."

Giving up on that bit of vengeance he went four miles off to the residence of John House. He selected a suitable place to camp and slept soundly until daybreak. All the next day he watched carefully but saw no sign of that particular enemy. Feeling that it must be John House's right to go on living, Sam waited until dark, then mounted his horse and started back to Greene County. Nobody had discovered him, and he had seen only the true friends who had provided him with food during his stay.

CHAPTER 5

Even worse difficulties lay ahead for the Hildebrand family as a result of the Vigilante mob's policy. The mob finally succeeded in obtaining the assistance of both the State and the Federal troops in causing as much havoc as they could. It was arranged for a Dutch company stationed at North Big River Bridge under Captain Esroger, another Dutch company stationed at Cadet under Captain Adolph, and a French company stationed at the Iron Mountain under Captain Flanche to join in a concerted plan to crush the whole Hildebrand family.

Emboldened by their success in assembling troops, the Vigilante mob marched boldly up to the original Hildebrand homestead. There they found Sam's mother reading her Bible, and notified her that she must immediately leave the county for it was their intention to burn her house and destroy all her property.

Sam's mother had always been a true Christian. She had always been kind and affectionate toward everybody. She had always been ready to relieve the distressed and assist the afflicted. Many a tearful person approaching death had been comforted by the pitying face of Mrs. Hildebrand, for she was the faithful friend at any sick-bed. For all the years that she had resided in that neighborhood she was known as one who spread loving kindness.

Imagine her shock when she was ordered to leave her home, the homestead built by her departed husband! In that home she had raised a large family. Every object in the house must have held a thousand sweet associations. As she considered all her years, seeking a cause for this misfortune, she certainly could find nothing that reproached her. As always in the past, she silently committed herself to God.

Hastily, she took her Bible and one bed from the house — nothing more. She arranged to have the bed moved to the home of her brother, Harvey McKee, who lived on Dry Creek in Jefferson County about thirty-five miles away. She burst into tears as she walked slowly through the little gate, knowing that she would never have a home of her own again.

It was generally known that her son Sam was the only one of her family who espoused the Rebel cause. Rank had been murdered without ever having expressed his opinion one way or the other, and Sam's brother William had joined the Union Army to fight until the close of the war. Washington took no part in the war at all; he was a peaceable and law-abiding citizen who never spoke a word that could be construed into any sympathy for the Southern cause. While the war was raging he carefully avoided making any mention of it. He was busily engaged in lead mining in the St. Joseph Lead mines three miles away from Big River Mills and about six miles from the family homestead. His partner, a man by the name of Landusky, was also loyal to the North and had been engaged to marry Sam's sister Mary. Her death, however, had prevented their marriage.

As for Sam's youngest brother, Henry, he was merely thirteen years old at this time, hardly an age to hold any political principles. He was still at home with his mother, doing the best he could to help her run the farm. Despite his youth he applied himself to his work very industriously.

On the 6th day of July, 1862, when Washington Hildebrand and Mr. Landusky were working in the drift underground, Captain Flanche and his cavalry company halted at the mine and ordered them to come out into the open. They immediately obeyed him. No questions were asked and no explanations were given.

Flanche ordered them to walk off a few steps toward a tree, which they did. He shouted the order, "Fire!", and his whole company fired at the two, literally tearing their bodies to pieces.

A citizen who happened to be present asked, "Why was this done?"

Flanche replied, carelessly driving off, "They bees the friends of Sam Hildebrand."

General John Sappington Marmaduke, leader of the Confederate cavalry west of the Mississippi River. He also saw service in Arkansas and Tennessee.
Kansas State Historical Society

Perhaps Captain Esroger wanted to place himself on an equal footing with Capt. Flanche, for he concluded that Sam Hildebrand's uncle, John Roan, would make a good target for proving that he himself could equal Flanche's brutality.

At that time John Roan was about fifty years of age and known throughout the country for his almost legendary honesty. He always paid his debts and kept himself aloof from both sides during the war, although nothing had ever been said to indicate that he was not loyal to the Union. As a matter of fact, one of his sons had joined the Union Army, although another was a Rebel. However, because he was the uncle of Sam and the father of Allen Roan there was plenty of pretext for Esroger's display of military brutality.

John Roan's house was situated about three miles from the St. Joseph Lead Mines and about the same distance from old Mrs. Hildebrand's ruined home. On the 10th day of July, 1862, Captain Esroger and his company rode up to John Roan's house. When the old man walked out on the porch to greet them, his white locks streaming in the wind, he had no suspicion at all that they came in a spirit other than friendship.

Esroger announced, "You are one tam prisoner."

Thereupon six men in the company were detailed to guard Roan as a prisoner and to march along slowly behind the contingent. They did so, and when they had covered above a mile from his house they commanded him to step off six paces. While his eyes were turned toward Heaven, his hands slightly raised in the attitude of prayer, the fatal word "Fire!" sounded. He fell to the ground, a mangled corpse.

There was still another actor in this bloody tragedy, and it seems that he had to tax his ingenuity to the utmost to find a way to outdo the atrocious acts of his two companions, Flanche and Esroger. This was Captain Adolph.

On the 23rd day of July, Adolph and his company, with some members of the Vigilante mob, went to Mrs. Hildebrand's house with the purpose of burning it. It was two stories high, built of handsomely cut stone and finished handsomely within. Altogether it was one of the best houses in the county.

First the soldiers broke down the picket fence and pitched the pieces into the house to be used as kindling. They refused to let the soldiers remove anything from the house, determined to destroy the furniture, clothing, bedding, and everything else under that roof. When everything was ready they set the kindling afire and joyously watched the flames spread. Before long the entire house was wrapped in a sheet of flames.

Mrs. Hildebrand's youngest son, Henry, along with an orphan boy who made his home with them to help in the cultivation of the farm, were present during the conflagration, and they looked on in bewilderment. Esroger turned to young Henry and commanded him to leave the place. Perhaps he meant to shoot the boy right on the spot, but it must have been clear that a young boy could never do anything to invite such treatment. As a matter of fact, Henry hardly understood the command, for he was gazing at the burning house, the only home he had ever known, and he must have felt more than bewildered.

Esroger once more ordered Henry to leave, but he remained staring in disbelief. Franklin Murphy, noticing that the boy did not understand the order was to be obeyed, watched as he slowly shook himself out of his stupor and mounted his horse. By the time he had ridden two hundred yards he was shot. He dropped out of the saddle, dead before he touched the ground.

The company went to the trouble of burning the large frame barn as well as the various cribs and stables on the premises. After that they claimed Henry's young friend, the orphan boy, and marched him off as their prisoner. The corpse of Henry lay untouched for several days, until some neighbors happened to find it and arrange a burial.

When news of all this reached Sam he was no longer able to soften his determination to retaliate. He sought evenge. He said to one of his friends, "The key of hell is not suffered to rust in the lock while I am on the war path."

CHAPTER 6

Perhaps one of the most miserable experiences that Sam always had to remember was witnessing the burning of his family's homestead. He had selected two good men, John Burlap and James Cato, to go with him on another excursion to St. François County in Missouri. They too had been badly treated at the outbreak of the war, and they too had many grievances to redress. Sam in complete sympathy, promised them any help he could give.

The three of them had by now obtained Federal uniforms. They started late in the afternoon of July 13th, 1862, and on reaching the river they discovered that the previous day's heavy rains had swelled it. They hesitated to ride into the turbid stream with all its floating driftwood, but decided that it was bad luck to turn back. They let their horses plunge into the stream and made the opposite shore without much difficulty. Burlap and Cato, while getting across, were somewhat scratched by the driftwood. On the opposite bank the three of them built a fire, dried their clothes, and took a snort from their black bottle. Then they camped until morning before continuing their journey.

When they reached the vicinity of Bloomfield in Stoddard County, Missouri, they met a man in civilian clothes and in a friendly conversation inquired, "Are there any Rebels in this vicinity?"

He replied, "There's a party of Rebels in Bloomfield, and they're tough customers. You'd better make your way back to Greenville, for otherwise you're sure to fall into their hands. I was with them all day, pretending that I wanted to enlist with them, so I learned all about their plans. I suspect that by tomorrow night they'll all be taken in."

Sam inquired, "Didn't they suspect you of being a spy?"

"No, they didn't," he answered. "I completely deceived them."

Sam then asked him, "Do you want to ride behind me for a spell, and then behind my partner here until we reach Greenville?"

He said, "Sure, if it's all right with you."

He sprang up behind Sam. After they had covered about two miles — not exactly in the direction of Greenville — Sam said, "I'm aiming to strike a certain cross road."

He didn't seem to offer any objection. He went on talking about his exploits as a spy, how he had learned the names of all the Rebels in Greenville and Fredericktown.

By this time Sam felt he had had enough, so he said frankly, "I'm Sam Hildebrand!" With that he knocked the stranger off his horse and shot him.

By this time Sam had fallen into such a habit of cruelty that he felt absolutely no compunction about killing. He just made a little notch underneath the stock of old "Kill-Devil."

From then on Sam and his friends traveled exclusively by night, carefully avoiding any act that would be likely to create a disturbance. They arrived safely at the home of Sam's brother-in-law on Flat River, within ten miles of the good old Hildebrand homestead where his mother had been evicted. Here for the first time he learned of the murder of his brother Washington and of his uncle John Roan. He knew that his mother had sought shelter with her brother in Jefferson County.

It seemed that his region was full of soldiers, and the Vigilante mob joyfully ran things their own way. Sam determined to go to Dry Creek to see his mother, although he knew that the soldiers were scouring the country for fifty miles around, planning his destruction particularly. They started at night and had to travel a circuitous route. Daylight overtook Sam and his companions within six miles of his uncle's home. They made a circuit around a hillside to look the land over, as was now their custom, then camped in such a position that they could be close to any pursuers for half an hour before they could be found.

Sam's companions slept while he kept watch. They had not been asleep very long before Sam discovered a party of men winding their way slowly in the semi-circle he and his companions had made. There were ten of them, all wearing the Federal uniform. Sam awakened his companions, and they observed the way they were slowly tracking them at a distance of about three hundred yards. As they watched they could hardly refrain from making war upon them, but Sam's main object at the moment was to see his mother, so he let those strangers pass on where the tracks they were following would lead them out of sight for a few minutes. Quickly, Sam and his friends mounted and rode on to another ridge, making a new camp within a quarter of a mile from the first attempted ambush. By that time the Federals had struck off in another direction, perhaps finding the tracks they were following a bit too fresh for their safety.

After dark Sam and his friends made their way cautiously through the woods to within a few hundred yards of his uncle's house. Dismounting, he left his horse with his comrades and approached the house. He even climbed upon a bee-gum to peep through one of the windows. Two strange men were seated in the room, and it seemed that a third man was there also.

As Sam leaned a little to one side to get a clearer view, the bee-gum tilted, throwing him with a desperate crash upon a pile of clapboards. He recovered in a hurry and in three bounds cleared the picket fence and deposited himself in the corner of the garden to await the result.

Of course the noise had aroused the inmates of the house, and they were soon outside with a light and a short double-barreled shotgun in the hands of Sam's uncle. While he inspected the damage done to his favorite bee-stand, he breathed out some rough threats against the villain who had attempted to steal his honey. After ordering his family and the two strangers back into the house, he posted himself in a fence corner about thirty yards off from where Sam was holding his breath. He was clearly ready to wage war against any offender.

The night was very dark, and Sam was afraid that if he should attempt to climb over the fence again the old man might pepper him with shot. He moved cautiously around to the back part of the garden and found an opening where a picket was missing. He squeezed through this aperture and crawled around to the rail fence where his uncle was. When Sam was at last within two panels of the old man he ventured to call him by name in a very low tone.

McKee recognized the voice and said, "Is that you, Sam?"

When Sam had answered he moved over to where his uncle was, and they shared a hearty handshake through a crack.

He told Sam, "The two men in the house right now are Union neighbors. They came over to tell me that the trail of a band of bushwhackers was discovered about six miles from there and that by tomorrow the whole country will be out in search of them. You better go back until my neighbors take their leave. After that come in to see your mother. She is well but continually grieving about her son Sam."

Sam returned to his companions and reported on his progress. Then he took his stand in the fence corner. As soon as the two neighbors were gone, his uncle made known to Mrs. Hildebrand and to his wife the cause of the disturbance earlier. The younger members of the family had retired by this time. Sam and his friends were invited into the house, and his mother started across the room toward him with a firm step. She tottered and might have fallen if he had not caught her in his arms. She rested her head on his chest, weeping like a child, and neither could Sam restrain his own tears.

His mother cried, "Oh, my dear son! Have you indeed come to see your mother in spite of the danger? I thought I would go down to the grave in sorrow without ever seeing you again."

Sam now would have gladly left war and revenge to others. He wanted to secret himself away in some quiet corner of the earth where, with his mother and his wife and children, he might once more take delight in the song of birds and the tranquil life he had enjoyed in his younger days.

After a little while Mrs. Hildebrand became calm again, and both she and Sam found satisfaction in talking together. His uncle now and then poked fun at Sam to lighten the moment.

He said, "Trying to steal my bee-gum, were you?"

His two daughters were busy in the kitchen preparing a supper, and there was really some gaiety until two o'clock, when Sam and his friends explained that they had to leave in order to make a safe retreat from the Vigilantes who surely would be searching for them at daylight.

Once outside, Sam led the way back over their former trail for half a mile to where they had crossed the creek. Now they rode in the water for about three miles to a public road heading south. They followed this for about six miles. Then, on reaching a rocky place where the horses would not leave tracks, they traveled into the woods for about two miles. They made their customary semi-circle around a hill and camped in a commanding position. Sam slept nearly all day while his companions did picket duty.

At nightfall they went calling on a friend who lived near Sam's former home, and learned from him that their trail had already been discovered. The whole militia force, composed of Sam's old enemies together with some Dutch regulars, were quartered at Big River Mills. It seemed that the woods were constantly being scoured, that each ford of the Big River was guarded night and day. Escape seemed impossible.

Before daylight they concealed their horses in a deep ravine covered with brush and briars. They themselves hid underneath a shelving rock near the top of a high bluff, from where they had a long-distance view of the Hildebrand homestead. The old house, they saw, was surrounded by soldiers, numerous enough to fill the yard and the adjoining enclosures. Suddenly Sam saw a dense column of smoke rise from the house, and realized that the vandals were burning the home of his childhood.

He saw the flames burst forth through the roof and lap out their long, fiery tongues at every window. He even saw the roof fall in, until all that remained were the massive, blackened stone walls. He wanted to throw himself upon those criminals and fight them until there wasn't a drop of life left in his veins. But that would have ended his hope of revenge, while his enemies would still be able to enjoy their pillage.

After dark that night, Sam and his friends returned to their hidden horses and commenced their retreat to Arkansas. Instead of going directly south they traveled west about twenty miles. When they struck the creek called Forche at Renault in Washington County they turned south. The route took them over the wild pine hills, west from Potosi. At night they camped in a secure place between Caledonia and Webster.

They had to continue their journey that evening, so just before sunset they raided a store for food. They collected all they wanted, including several bottles of "burst-head." Traveling all night, following Black River down to Current River which they crossed at Carter's Ferry, they made their way safely to Greene County, Arkansas.

CHAPTER 7

Sam remained a few days at headquarters, then commenced making plans for another trip against his enemies at Big River. He had not as yet heard about the killing of his young brother Henry, and all he knew about the burning of his mother's home was what he had seen from a distance as the flames rose. Foolishly, he confided in a few men about his plan to retaliate. One of those listening at the time was Thomas Haile, called Devilish Tom, who had just been spinning some of his amusing yarns.

When Sam happened to mention the name of Franklin Murphy Tom showed an instant interest, and proposed to go along to see some of his old friends at Big River. They set out with another man and passed through Stoddard, then into Wayne County where Sam wanted to look up a man named Stokes who had fed him on previous trips. Naturally, Sam was grateful to him and admired him. Shortly after this, however, Sam learned that Stokes was laying plans for his capture and had already put the Federals on his trail. Just the same, Sam was unwilling to kill Stokes until he was absolutely sure that he was guilty. He claimed that he was not willing to fall into the error that was so common among the Federals of killing an innocent man only to gratify the personal animosity of some informer.

Just after dark Sam went to the Stokes house alone and was

pleased to be treated in a very cordial manner.

"Well, Mr. Hildebrand," he said. "I'm glad to see you, and I hope you are still too smart for the Feds."

Sam asked, "Are there any Feds in Greenville?"

"None, sir, none at all. I was there today. The place is entirely clear of the scamps. By the way, Mr. Hildebrand, are you alone?"

"Oh, yes. I am taking this trip by myself."

And Stokes returned, "Glad to assist you, sir. You must stay with me tonight, and I'll hide you tomorrow in a safe place. You can go on tomorrow night if you like, although I'd like you to stay longer if you want to."

Sam replied, "Thank you, but I've troubled you enough in the past and I stopped in tonight just to tell you that I appreciate your past kindness. I'm expected at a friend's home about a mile off, and I'll stay with him until tomorrow night."

Then Sam went back to where he had left his two traveling companions. After they had donned the Federal uniform, they rode around the place and approached Stokes' house from another direction. Riding up to his door in a great hurry they called, "Mr. Stokes, Mr. Stokes!"

When he appeared at the door Tom Haile in a very confidential tone offered this: "Well, sir! We are on the hot trail of Sam Hildebrand. He robbed a man down on the Greenville road, five miles below here, about sunset time. We know he came in this direction, so we decided to ride over here to ask if you've seen or heard anything of him."

Stokes heartily replied, "I reckon I have, by George! Sam Hildebrand was here not more than an hour ago, and I tried to detain him. He was alone, and he said he was going to stay until tomorrow night at a certain house. Wait a minute! I'll get my gun and coat and go along with you. We've got him this time, sure."

"All right," said Tom. "Come along. We are always glad to meet a man of your stripe."

Stokes marched along with the boys until they came to where Sam was waiting for them. On coming up to Sam in the dim light he asked, "How many men have you?"

Tom replied, "Twelve."

Standing in the dark Stokes at once began laying plans for Sam's capture, relating what he had done on previous occasions to capture Sam Hildebrand, "but that Sam was too sharp for me."

Just then out of the dark Sam stopped him by announcing, "I am Sam Hildebrand myself."

Immediately Sam emptied the Kill-Devil into Stokes' chest.

The three men proceeded traveling through the night. At daybreak they arrived near the ruins of the Hildebrand Homestead and called at the home of an old friend. Knowing that they were in enemy country and in danger of being trailed, they were of course unable to sleep. It was also impossible for them to travel in daylight, for they were 150 miles beyond safety. They knew that the government had no less than 500 men in active service for the special purpose of capturing Sam. Hiding their horses in a thicket under a bluff, they entered a nearby cave — a cave which was afterwards known as the Sam Hildebrand Cave.

The friend they had called upon remained in the cave for a while, giving them the particulars of the atrocities daily committed by the Federal troops, even to the point of explaining how they had murdered Sam's innocent young brother Henry. At this Sam was in a worse state of misery than ever, realizing that all his brothers had been slain in cold blood except for William who had joined the Federal army. Unfortunately, his well-known loyalty had not been enough to shield his neutral brothers from butchery.

After studying the matter for several hours Sam finally made up his mind. He determined to sell his life as dearly as possible. He would wage a war of fire and blood against his persecutors — "while one should last" — until his own death.

Only one word escaped his lips: "Revenge!" and that word resounded in the cavern. He rushed toward the mouth of the cave, but the two men he was traveling with sprang to hold him back. Just the same, he managed to dash down a steep declivity and mount his horse. Tom Haile followed, and before Sam could ride around a fallen tree he had Sam's horse by the bridle.

"Hold on, Sam! Don't be a fool. If you're going to throw your life away you won't be able to kill your enemies. If you take your time you may be able to wreak your revenge. If I go back without you what shall I tell your wife and children? Come, Sam, you must not forget your duty to them."

Afterwards Sam had no recollection of alighting and returning to the cave, for he was actually out of his mind with grief. When he awoke it was nearly sunset, and Tom soon had him laughing in spite of himself.

In the depth of the night they moved on about five miles and stopped at the residence of William Patton, a man Sam especially wanted to kill. Patton was at home when they arrived, but by some means he eluded their grasp. They slipped out, and before daylight they had hidden their horses in a thicket on Turkey Run, a small creek that emptied into Big River above Addison Murphy's. They stationed themselves near the residence of Joe McGahan; by morning they decided it was fruitless to watch for him any longer and moved on.

Sam said, "Let's repair to Franklin Murphy's home, for it's not more than a mile from here."

Tom made another suggestion: "Let's return to our horses and plan our future movements carefully."

When they were with their horses Sam suggested stirring up Franklin Murphy because he had been present at the burning of his mother's house and certain other incidents that had led him to suspect his conduct, but Tom dissuaded him. Tom insisted, "I don't believe Franklin Murphy had anything to do with the burning of your mother's house. He could never have rescued your brother Frank from the hands of that mob who believed they had the sanction of public opinion. He could never have prevented an army of soldiers, acting under the command of another man, from burning down the house. He had nothing to do with the killing of your brother Henry. It will never do for you to harm Franklin Murphy. He is a member of an Order that dates back many thousands of years. The members are bound together to shield one another, and they are powerful people."

Tom sounded so sincere and looked so serious that Sam assured him, "I'll never harm one of them except in self-defense."

At this point Sam was willing to be persuaded to return to Arkansas. They passed through Farmington and Fredericktown on the following night, then camped in the woods until evening. They started before nightfall in order to capture some fresh horses.

Dressed in their Federal uniforms they were riding along a Madison County road when they saw a fine-looking horse in a nearby lot. Sam dismounted and went up to the horse to catch him, but he was shy and kept his head as far from Sam's hand as possible. While he was trying to get a halter on the spirited animal a woman stepped out on the porch and cried out, "See here! What are you trying to do?"

"I'm trying to catch this horse," Sam replied.

She cried out, "Let him alone, you good-for-nothing! Don't you look pretty, you miserable scamp, trying to steal my only horse!"

"Yes, Madame, but I'm afraid you are a Rebel."

"Yes, I am a Rebel, sir, and proud of it! I have two sons in the Rebel army, and if I had six more they should all be in it. You white-livered, insignificant scum of creation! You had better let my horse alone. Why, you are worse than Sam Hildebrand! He wouldn't take the last horse from a poor widow woman!"

By this time Sam had caught the horse, but at that speech by the woman he pulled the halter off, begged her pardon, and left.

Tom never let him forget about that adventure.

CHAPTER 8

While Sam was recruiting at Rebel headquarters in Greene County, Arkansas, Captain Bolin and most of his men returned for a needed rest. Time passed rapidly, with conversation active enough to keep everyone entertained.

After a thorough rest, on the 25th of August, Sam selected three men and started back to St. François County in Missouri. They met with no unusual circumstances until they arrived in Madison County. Within eight miles of Fredericktown, daylight overtook them and they stopped at an old friend's house for breakfast. Sam had stopped there on previous trips, and this time he was assured that there were no Federal troops in the neighborhood. Feeling free because of this advice, Sam decided to spend that day on a journey to his old home on Big River.

After eating breakfast and feeding their horses, the three men made their way to their usual crossing place on the gravel road leading from Pilot Knob to Fredericktown. Suddenly they were fired upon from the brush by about fifty soldiers.

Fortunately they had not traveled by the path that crossed the road at the place where the soldiers were stationed in ambush. They were about 200 yards away, and the firing did not kill any of the three travelers. However, Sam's horse was shot from under him. The ball pierced the horses's chest, passing through Sam's pantaloons and slightly burning his knee.

At Sam's word, his three men whirled into the brush, retreating in the direction from which they had come. Sam was on foot and a bit lame from the effects of the wound received at Flat Woods as well as from the burning of his knee. Still, they moved fast, escaping to a distance of about a mile before they stopped. Sam ordered his men to hitch their horses in a thicket which could be held in case they were followed.

After waiting for some time and hearing no signs of pursuit, Sam decided to return cautiously to where they had been fired upon, hoping they might be able to get in a few shots of their own. They crept up slowly. Six or seven men were actually near the place, but could not be safely approached. In an effort to get closer, Sam and his men made their way in the direction of Pilot Knob for about a mile. Then they crossed the gravel road from behind a hill and approached the soldiers from the opposite side.

Sam got sight of the enemy just in time to see a party ride up, leading three horses. Deciding that he and his men could get no closer without exposing themselves, Sam decided to try at long range. At the first crack of Kill-Devil one man got a heavy ball which killed him. At this his party turned to follow Sam's party into the woods, for which they paid dearly. Their dash caused Sam and his men to scatter in different directions, each taking a separate course through the woods in the roughest places they could find. This rendered it difficult for the Feds to follow. Sam and his men stopped at every place they could find which gave them a chance to get a pop at the soldiers, then shifted in a different direction. This afforded old Kill-Devil a chance to howl from many a dense thicket in the wild woods until midnight, when the strangers gave up the chase and quit the unequal fight.

Sam's men met at the top of a certain high hill that had been designated in the morning. He had four new notches on the stock of old Kill-Devil, two of his men had killed one man apiece, and the other had wounded one. By this time the Federals started their search with three or four hundred men. Their numbers were so great that Sam's small brigade remained hidden. That night, during a heavy rain, Sam and his followers went into Fredericktown and managed to steal a horse apiece, but they did not get saddles and bridles because of their hurry. Before morning they had covered thirty miles on their way back to Arkansas, all four riding bareback with only a halter for a bridle.

They made a stop at the place where they had enjoyed a breakfast on the way up, suspicious that their host on that occasion had deceived them in regard to soldiers in the area. Perhaps he had even reported the movement of Sam and his friends, for it was true that a lad of about fifteen years of age had ridden off while Sam and the others were eating their breakfast. They wanted to settle with the old man, but it turned out he was not at home. Sam at least helped himself to a saddle and a bridle, then returned to Arkansas, leaving the Federals to continue looking for the sharpshooters who had given them such a bad time.

Before reaching Arkansas they made a detour of about twenty miles to lay in their winter supplies. They knew of a certain Union man who, from his home at the crossroads, had caused the expulsion of two families by reporting them as Rebels. He still had the remnants of what was once a prosperous country store. Sam rode up to his door at sunset. One of his men remained outside to prevent anyone from leaving. The crusty old fellow in the store was not disposed to be accommodating, but Sam collected everything that could be put upon the horses and upon a mule they "borrowed".

"Charge it all to Uncle Sam," Sam told him.

Before morning they were out of danger. Upon reaching camp they relieved the needy, not forgetting the two families that "Old Crusty" had driven from his neighborhood.

CHAPTER 9

Sam's wife and children were still living in Cook settlement, in St. François County, Missouri, and that was enemy country. He could not pay them a visit without bringing ruin upon them if anyone should ever spread the news to the Unionists. He was determined, though, to effect their escape to Arkansas as soon as possible. Captain Bolin and his men promised their co-operation at any time he could arrange a plan.

Sam said, "Of course the whole force would be insufficient if such an object should be attempted, for two or three thousand men could be brought against me in less than twenty-four hours." Still, he kept himself posted on the strength of the enemy along the route and in the latter part of September, he started another raid into Missouri along with three of Quantrill's men. Upon arriving at the St. Francis River they found it flooded, but they did not halt on that account.

On the second day after leaving the main road they made a detour that would enable them to travel during the day. When they came within sight of a house they saw someone running into the yard. Immediately afterward they saw a little boy running out of the house toward the barn. Sam and his men dashed forward and surrounded the barn. Through a crack they saw a man hiding within the barn, and they demanded his surrender. He appeared in the doorway with his hands raised.

They took him back into the barn and soon discovered that his bundle contained a Federal uniform. The citizen's clothes he was wearing were much too small for him. It was promptly decided that he was a Federal spy. They searched him and found a letter in his pocket from a man named Scaggs, addressing the authorities at Fredericktown. It contained the names of several Rebel neighbors whom he was expected to burn out.

Sam happened to know one name on the list, and therefore he took it for granted that Scaggs lived in the neighborhood of that person. They led the spy out for half a mile and shot him. Thereupon, changing their course, they went in search of Scaggs. It was after dark before they located his residence.

Dressed in Federal uniforms, Sam and his companions rode up to the gate, called Scaggs out, arrested him and led him to the house of a friend who explained that Scaggs had already made two widows in that neighborhood by reporting their husbands as rebels. Sam and his Quantrill friends took him along with them and at daylight hung him from a limb in the woods. After that they made their way toward Castor Creek in Madison County.

The following night, after crossing Castor Creek, they discovered a camp of Federals about twenty or thirty strong. Sam and his companions decided to charge them but, to their surprise, they turned out to be three or four times as numerous as they had seemed. Though they charged on through as quickly as possible, two of their horses were killed as they flew by, and one of their own number was slightly wounded in the fleshy part of his thigh.

They were lucky indeed to get through that camp, and they captured four pickets who had been placed in a lane on the opposite side. They mistook Sam's gang for their own men at first. The two men who had lost their mounts were given new horses by the pickets who then explained that they were Leeper's men. Sam thereupon shot them and hurried on. Later, when they returned through this area, they were told by the citizens that they had killed five and wounded several others in that charge through the camp — bringing the total to nine killed, including the pickets.

It was clear that the wounded man in Sam's group could not be kept in Missouri safely. It would mean death to any man under whose roof the wounded man took refuge. The host would and all his property burned. His wife and children would be turned out, forlorn and destitute. To avoid bringing such a calamity upon any of their friends, the wounded man had to make his way alone back to Arkansas.

Sam and the other two left him to his own devices and traveled the remainder of the night in the direction of St. François County. They were later told that during the following day they had been trailed, but a rainfall at sunrise destroyed their tracks. On the following night they managed to reach the home of a friend near the ruins of what had once been Sam's home. Here Sam remained for two whole days and nights, resting, scouting, and trying to shoot some of the miscreants who belonged to the old mob. However, he really had no chance at them.

At this time Sam and his companions were nearly accosted by the mob which had assumed the name of Militia with James Craig as their captain. Sam got a bead on Craig as he came riding very fast, and for the only time in its history the Kill-Devil failed. Sam was lucky to get away unrecognized.

On returning to the home of his friend near his own former home, Sam learned that the horses he and his companions had concealed in a nook in the bluffs along the Big River had been discovered by some boys out hunting. They had reported this find to the Militia. As soon as they learned this, Sam and his men started toward the place they had left their horses and fortunately found them safe. Since, it seemed, their trip had not given them any satisfaction, they decided to obtain supplies from their good Union friends before leaving the area.

They reached Flat River about the middle of the afternoon and rode up to the store that was kept by the sons of John Bean, a member of the Vigilante mob. He himself was not present, and the boys had sense enough not to make any demonstration. Without damaging anything whatsoever, Sam and his friends helped themselves to anything they needed — as Sam later said, "in part payment for (his own) property which had been destroyed." He realized that John Bean's sons considered these strangers bad customers, and they didn't even take the trouble to book the articles taken.

When the Militia received news of this foray, they mustered their whole force and, on the following day, struck Sam's trail and overtook his men between Pilot Knob and Fredericktown. They followed for about ten miles and got sight of the travelers only when they had to pass over the tops of hills. As night fell the followers were no longer seen or heard.

Sam and his gang traveled all night and, at daylight, rode up to the house owned by a man named Slater in the southern part of Wayne County, Missouri. He had been on their list for quite some time, for since the beginning of the war he had been reporting Southern men. In fact, he had succeeded in having several of them imprisoned and their families impoverished. He happened to be at home, and at sight of his uninvited guests the man wilted "like a cabbage leaf," as Sam later expressed it. They dragged him about a mile away and shot him.

Pursuing their way back to Greene County, Sam and his friends divided their spoils among the destitute families who had been driven there by the ruthless hands of Northern sympathizers.

CHAPTER 10

The worst elements in the Vigilante mob soon formed a militia company with James Craig as captain and Joe McGahan first lieutenant, as already mentioned. Craig could neither read nor write, and therefore the first lieutenant was actually at the head of the marauders. By becoming a militia company they merely legalized their acts of plunder. They did not pretend to take the field against the Rebels or to strike any blow in defense of the state. While drawing pay from the Government, they spent their time hunting hogs, sheep, and cattle belonging to other people.

They had killed all of Sam's brothers except the one who had joined the Union army (where they could not reach him) and they carefully divided the Hildebrand property among themselves. Mrs. Hildebrand had originally been a Union sympathizer, but they had driven her off to Jefferson County with nothing but her bed and her Bible. The homestead had been burned, yet there was an abundance of stock belonging to the estate and a large field of standing corn. They collected the stock and gathered the corn and divided it among themselves. During this division they naturally had a number of disagreements among themselves. A question arose as to whether an officer was entitled to more than a private, and a few men went home declaring that they would not have anything if they could not have their fair share.

At the very time this valorous militia company had stacked their muskets against the fence and were chasing Mrs. Hildebrand's sheep and pigs around through the dog fennel, Sam was capturing a government train and getting his supplies in what he considered an honorable manner. It was the first of November, 1862, when Sam learned that the Federals were in the habit of hauling their army supplies to Bloomfield from Cape Girardeau on the Mississippi River. Captain Bolin and Sam determined to lay in their own supplies from the same source.

They took ten men and carried about ten days' rations. Arriving on a stream called White Water which, with Castor Creek, formed the Eastern fork of the St. Francis River, they concealed themselves in an unfrequented part of the woods. It was necessary for them to keep thoroughly posted in regard to the expected time of the train and the probable strength of the escort. Dressed as a country farmer, Sam undertook this delicate mission and pretended to be searching for a stray mule. He made his way on foot to the vicinity of the mill and concealed himself near a road to await the arrival of someone on the way to the mill.

When a man came along with a cart and oxen, Sam let him pass, fearing that any questions might arouse suspicion.

After waiting for about an hour he saw a boy coming along slowly in the distance, riding on his sack and whistling little fragments of "John Brown's Body." Sam stepped into the road before he got near and walked along until they met. Sam asked him, "Have you by any chance seen my lost mule?" He claimed never to have seen such an animal.

Sam then said, "Well, I guess I won't go searching any longer. But I'm anxious to get back to Bloomfield if I can only get a ride somehow, for I'm tired out from walking so much."

The boy then said, "The government wagons are passing here tomorrow, and maybe you can get a ride."

Sam said, "Well, I'd be afraid to do that, for the Rebels might capture me."

The boy said, "There's no danger of that, for twenty soldiers always go along with the wagons."

Sam returned to his comrades with the information they wanted, so they finished their arrangements for the attack. After dark they turned up the road along which the wagons were to pass. They selected a place called the Round Pond and hid in a clump of heavy timber. Since the soldiers would not be able to see through this clump, they would imagine that the woods were full of Rebels.

Night passed, and the morning hours wore away. At length they saw two government wagons coming, and in the sunlight twenty bayonets gleamed. Suddenly Sam and his pals broke from the woods with a great shout. They dashed among the soldiers with all the noise they could make. They fired a few shots, killing two and causing the remainder to break for the woods in every direction. Because the sole object of this trip was to get supplies of clothing, ammunition, and so on, Sam and his men made no attempt to pursue the escort.

They unhitched the horses and packed them with such things as they needed, then burned the wagons and whatever they could not take with them.

The way back to their own camp led through Mingo Swamp. They made their way safely to the St. Francis River, but found it greatly flooded. With a great deal of difficulty they managed to swim the river with their booty. One man named Banks became tangled in a drift of grapevines and brush and drowned before the other men could reach him.

On their return to headquarters, the men busied themselves for several weeks building houses for comfortable use during the coming winter. Their headquarters were on Crawley's Ridge, between the St. Francis River and Cash Creek in Greene County, Arkansas. It afforded a safe retreat from a large army encumbered with artillery.

Many of Captain Bolin's men had their families with them, and this little community soon presented a view of neatness and comfort. Unfortunately, scouts were constantly bringing fresh rumors of barbarous acts committed by the various Federal bands that infested Southeast Missouri, making it their special aim to arrest, burn out, shoot and destroy all those peaceable citizens who had never taken part in the war.

Especially marked out for extinction were those who had been known to shelter "Sam Hildebrand the Bushwhacker." If any man should see such a person passing along the road and then fail to report the same to headquarters, regardless of the distance, he was taken out of his house and shot, without even the shadow of a trial to ascertain whether he was guilty or not. One old man who had served his country in many a hard-fought battle before his tormentors were born and who now hoped to settle down to a life of peace and security, found himself suddenly condemned and shot for disloyalty, because he generously took into his home for the night a stranger who afterwards proved to be "the notorious Sam Hildebrand."

Around the first day of December, 1862, Captain Bolin, Sam, and nine other men mounted and started on another trip. They crossed the St. Francis and traveled until they reached West Prairie in Scott County, Missouri, where they came upon a squad of thirty Federals. They seemed to imagine themselves perfectly safe, for they had not placed any pickets. Sam and his company ran upon them, and before they had time to fight at all they were so badly demoralized that they could not remember how. Four of them were killed, several more were wounded. Sam's men charged through the camp and in half an hour returned to renew the attack, but by that time there was nobody left to fight.

In the first charge the Rebels caused several horses to break loose, though these were later caught. Of their own, one man was wounded, shot through the thigh with a Minnie ball. Captain Bolin and six men took the wounded man back with them to Arkansas, while Henry Resinger, George Lasiter, and Sam set out on a trip to St. François County.

One morning at daybreak these men found themselves on the gravel road leading from Pilot Knob to Fredericktown, about seven miles from the latter. Concealing themselves in a thicket, they watched the road until evening before spotting any enemy. A squad of Federals came along, riding very fast, and Sam hailed them to cause a momentary halt; they fired. One of the riders fell to the ground, but the others hastened on until they were out of sight. While Sam and his men were examining the dead man, they saw three more advancing from a distance, trying to overtake those who had preceded them.

Sam and his party divided in order to be able to attack from two different places, but as the men approached they were seen not to be in Federal uniforms. After they were taken prisoners it was ascertained that they were Southern sympathizers from near Fredericktown. They had been imprisoned at the Knob for several weeks. Now, having been released, they were on their way home. Sam was asking them about the forces at the different military posts when the group of Union soldiers on whom Sam and his party had fired shortly before came riding back with a much larger force. Suddenly Sam's group was nearly surrounded by a broken and scattered line at a distance of only a hundred yards. Here they were, only three surrounded by sixty.

Sam called to his men, "Follow me!" and dashed for the incomplete part of the circle. The enemies attempted to close the line, but when Sam had started toward that point he had not the least intention of getting out that way. He wheeled and rushed toward the rear, followed by his own men, shooting as they ran. Soon they had gained distance in the woods and were able to take advantage of the darkness closing upon them. Being on foot, they escaped while the cavalry became tangled in the brush.

Luckily Sam's contingent escaped unhurt, although more than fifty shots had been fired at them. Sam had received two bullet holes through the rim of his hat and one through the sleeve of his coat; one of his men got a notch in his whiskers. They were not certain whether they had hurt any of the Federals as they escaped. They kept together and returned to their hidden horses, then rode back through the brush to get a few more shots at the Federals at long range. But they had left the spot.

Sam and his group made their way on toward Fredericktown but they saw no more soldiers. During the night they visited several friends. At the time there were only two men in the area whom the Rebels wanted to hang, and they happened not to be at home. The following day they tore down the telegraph wire on the road to Pilot Knob and stationed themselves about a mile from town in order to bushwack the Federals when they came by to mend the wire. By this time the Federals were learning from experience, however, so they sent out some Southern sympathizers to do the mending, and they were not molested.

Sam made a deal with one of the sympathizers for ammunition, and in the evening when the wire had again been torn down, he was the one who came to fix it and he supplied Sam with the powder and lead requested. It was learned from this man that a general movement against the Rebels was to be made by the troops both at Fredericktown and the Knob on the following day. At this time the whole country between there and Arkansas was in the hands of the Federals. They had been accustomed to the Rebel tactic of making a back movement toward Arkansas immediately after creating an excitement. Sam now turned north, planning to wait a few days until the southern woods were completely scoured and thus rendered safe.

During this intermission Sam hunted up a man by the name of Cunningham who had been living in the vicinity of Bloomfield. He had once professed to be a strong Southern man and had been of some service to the Rebels as a spy. During the second year of the Rebellion, though, he changed his plans and became a dangerous enemy of the Rebels. He was zealous in reporting both citizens and soldiers to the Federal authorities.

Sam now planned to arrest him and take him to Colonel Jeffries' camp, ten miles south of Bloomfield, so that he might be dealt with by the Colonel as he saw proper. On gaining the vicinity of Farmington, where Cunningham then lived, Sam learned that he was carrying on these measures with a high hand and was very abusive to those whom he had in his power. It was said that he even robbed his own brother,

Burril Cunningham, and allowed him to be abused unmercifully by a squad of men under his command.

On reaching the Valley Forge, Sam and his men struck Cunningham's trail and followed on toward Farmington. Some Federals seemed to be on their trail and they could have overtaken Sam's group if a friend had not deceived them in regard to the course Sam had taken.

Sam found Cunningham at his own house. When he approached the door and demanded his surrender, Cunningham attempted to draw a revolver and Sam shot him through the heart.

They now returned to Bloomfield and reported to Colonel Jeffries, with whom they remained for about three weeks.

On the 5th day of January, 1863, Captain Reuben Barnes requested Sam to assist him in capturing a man by the name of Captain Walker, who had charge of a Federal contingent and was now supposed to be at his home about six miles from there.

As Sam and his men approached the house they saw Walker running out with a pistol in each of his hands. They were near enough for Sam to call out, ordering him to surrender. At this Walker came nearer to them. Suddenly he shot Captain Barnes and started to run away. Sam shot him dead instead of giving chase.

They carried Captain Barnes back to Bloomfield where he died the same day. Sam then returned to Greene County, Arkansas, where the whole regiment was going into winter quarters.

CHAPTER 11

On the 23rd of January, 1863, Sam started alone on a trip to Missouri, for the purpose of making arrangements for the escape of his family to Arkansas. The second night, as he was riding over a brushy ridge, he was suddenly hailed by a cry of "Who comes there?"

In an instant he became aware of his close proximity to a Federal camp. He wheeled his horse into the woods to the right, dashed furiously down a steep hill for a short distance and, in the darkness, plunged over a precipice that was eight or ten feet high. The horse fell among some rocks and was killed. Sam himself was precipitated a few feet further into a deep hole filled with water from some creek.

Although he was considerably confused at first, he did have sense enough to crawl up out of the water. As he stood there dripping, he heard some soldiers dashing down the hill toward him. He crossed the creek and ran up the opposite hillside. He could have made his escape except for the fact that he had left his gun in the deep hole, and he could not bear to leave his beloved Kill-Devil.

Within a few moments the soldiers, evidently not seeing him or guessing what had happened, went back to their earlier positions. Sam slipped back cautiously and jumped into the water to recover the gun. He had to wade up to his chin while his feet felt around for the gun. Finally he got his foot under it and raised it, but he had no sooner gotten it in his hands than he saw five or six soldiers returning with a light.

They were making their way through a crevice in the bluff, some steps above the rock from which Sam had fallen. He had just time enough to wade down the creek which was only a few inches deep in places. He secreted himself behind a cluster of willows that hung over the edge of the steep bank about twenty yards below.

The Federals remained for ten or fifteen minutes, walking around the dead horse and around the water hole. They threw the glare of their lantern in every direction. Though Sam was completely hidden as he stood there in the water, shivering with cold, holding his dripping gun, he felt more like anything else in the world than a major. Fortunately the soldiers struck the trail he had made in going up the hill with dripping clothes, and they went in pursuit.

Taking this opportunity, Sam slowly left his retreat and waded stealthily down the creek for a long distance. Climbing up the hill on the same side where the Federals were camped, he made a circuit around them and reached a road some four or five miles ahead. He walked rapidly to keep himself warm. Just before the break of day he arrived at the house of a man he knew. Though wet, hungry, and on foot, he was soon supplied with everything he needed. His gun was cleaned and by the time the full morning spread over the land Kill-Devil looked brighter than usual.

When Sam set out in the direction of Fredericktown he fell in with twenty-five Rebel boys under the command of Lieutenant Childs. Childs asked Sam to take command of his men in order to give the Federals a "whack" at Bollinger's Mill on Castor Creek. That locality for some time had been a place of rendezvous for Southern recruits, and so the Federals always had some of their own men stationed there. Often they were 150 strong, but Sam agreed to lead the way on condition the young men would take an oath never to surrender under any circumstances.

After that oath was administered they marched along, arriving at Bollinger's Mill at about eleven o'clock on the night of February 4th. They succeeded in capturing the pickets and then made a charge on their camp. There was a furious fight for about five minutes (or until the Federals got ready to fight). By that time twenty-two of their number had been killed, and when Sam gave the signal his young fellows marched out double-quick, taking along four prisoners. Some information was pumped out of them, but they were released when Sam determined they were not McNeal's men. One of his own men, Henry Resinger, had been killed and three who were wounded were

General Sterling Price, governor of Missouri from 1853 to 1857, assumed command of the Missouri Militia in May, 1861, and took command of the Missouri State Guard July 20, 1861.

Kansas State Historical Society

carried away in the retreat. At daylight they all set out for Mingo Swamp.

The Federals followed. Sam's outfit was slowed down on account of the wounded. The Federals made their way around and charged, striking Sam's column at right angles. They divided the retreating line, cutting off seven men whom they took as prioners. In this latter little skirmish Sam lost one man and killed three Federals. After that they fell back so they were able to make their way to the St. Francis River, which they had to swim. One horse was drowned but the men got safely over.

They struck camp and prepared a meal that turned out to be breakfast, dinner, and supper all in one. Suddenly they heard someone calling from the opposite shore, "Bring me a horse!"

From his voice they knew him to be William Cato, one of the seven who had been taken prisoner. One of the other men swam over to him with a horse, and when he arrived in camp he reported that six of the men taken prisoner had been shot, that he had made his escape by dodging into the brush. He was barefooted and had torn off nearly all his clothing. Afterward it was learned that the officer in command at Bollinger's Mill was Captain Leeper from Ironton, Missouri.

Sam did not remain but one week in camp. Then, selecting two men to go along with him, he started back to Missouri to make another effort to move his family to Arkansas. When they arrived at Fredericktown they found the place full of soldiers. There was one resident, a Dutchman, whose meddlesome disposition led him to put soldiers on the track of private citizens. He was known never to leave town, and therefore it would be impossible to kill him in secret.

Sam took advantage of the dark night, left off his coat and, selecting a saw buck that he found at a wood pile, walked up to that man's front door. On being told he was not at home Sam returned to where his two men were waiting and left town as soon as possible, headed for Farmington. At the first sign of daylight they left the road for several miles, secreting themselves on a certain hill because a friend on whom they had called during the night had told them that the military authorities were aware of Sam's presence in the neighborhood and had secured two or three good woodsmen to track him.

About one o'clock that afternoon Sam and his two men discovered a man slowly tracking around the steep hill, looking about cautiously, holding his gun in a position to fire suddenly. Because the ground was hard and the horses were not easily trailed, he was moving along very slowly. It was hard to decide whether he was a brave man or a natural fool. Sam made his way a bit down the hill and wounded him severely in order to make his presence known. He yelled so loud that

Sam had to finish him with his knife. That brought other horsemen, so Sam and his friends hid in a thicket on Wolf Creek, near the residence of John Griffin.

At this place Sam learned that his wife had procured a little wagon and a yoke of oxen with which to move to Arkansas. She had started out with the family on February 16th and by this time must have been in the vicinity of Bloomfield.

During the night, Sam and his men went out on the plank road leading from Farmington to Ste. Genevieve and fired into a camp of Federals. They could not get near enough to harm them, but they wanted to draw them out to hunt them. That little trick did not work, and they had to give up. They went on to the junction of the Pilot Knob and Iron Mountain roads. There they robbed a store that belonged to a Dutchman by the name of Abright, and they started back toward Arkansas with all the goods they could pack.

At this point of the war the Federals had possession of all the principal places in Southeast Missouri, including Bloomfield. There was no doubt in Sam's mind that his family were now in their hands. He and his men were passing through Stoddard when they discovered the Federals about to overtake them. In fact they were so close that they had to throw off a part of their loads in order to ride rapidly enough to outrun them.

Upon arriving at the St. Francis River they found it heavily guarded. Their only chance was to whip the Federals, and they decided to try. First retreating into a dense cane brake they started shooting. They killed three men on the second round, and then the rest fled. Sam and his men managed to get home safely, with enough booty to be able to supply clothes and food for their friends.

CHAPTER 12

In the hope of getting his family to Arkansas safely Sam made the trip to Bloomfield, although that place was held by a large Federal force under McNeal. He set out with three good men and crossed the St. Francis River at a shoal. They had proceeded about ten miles when they ran into a company of McNeal's men. Of course they were immediately fired upon, and one of Sam's men was slightly wounded in the fleshy part of his arm. They thought it best to retreat from the firing of nearly a hundred enemy soldiers, and they did. They were pursued, but at too great a distance to be shot.

Wanting to get a few shots at them, Sam and his men crossed the river, plunging their horses in the deep water at the nearest point, swimming. They had nearly gained the opposite shore when the Federals ran onto the bank they had just left and fired a volley at them with muskets. Their shots were all too high.

Sam and his men reached the bank where the willows were thick. They jumped off their horses and returned the fire. They were able to see that three of the enemy group were killed, but the enemy kept up a random fire at the willow thicket and wounded three of the horses in Sam's party. That caused the horses to run up into the woods, terribly frightened. The enemy across the river took refuge behind trees in order to watch what was happening on the other shore. In that position they stood two rounds from Sam's rifles, and four of them fell, having been shot in the head.

Before Sam could get in another shot he noticed that a portion of the enemy was making its way up the river, evidently with the intention of engaging attention at that place while another group could attack in surprise. He and his men retreated and were able to find a safe place where they could remain all night. The next morning they discovered that the Federals had gone on to Bloomfield, having secured a wagon and team from an old man living nearby for the purpose of hauling off their dead. The old man told Sam that there had been seven killed and two wounded in that Federal camp.

Sam now decided to try his luck on foot. No doubt by stealthy movements he could find his family and help them get to Arkansas. Actually, in a few days he did meet his family about twenty miles south of Bloomfield, in an old wagon pulled by a yoke of oxen. His wife was driving, and after the joyous reunion she told him that Captain Bolin's men had removed her from Flat Woods to Bloomfield in Stoddard County, Missouri, but that McNeal, on taking posssession of the town, had ordered her to leave. He claimed that "the wife and family of that desperado, Sam Hildebrand, could not remain within 100 miles of his headquarters."

With the wagon and oxen furnished her by a friend to the Rebel cause, she had taken the children and some provisions out upon the road, making her way as best she could and preparing to camp for the night in the woods. Upon meeting with Sam she was able to give him some information about the two or three squads of Federals she had seen that day.

On the following morning the reunited family resumed the journey. About ten o'clock six Union soldiers came suddenly upon them at a short turn in the road. Because Sam was wearing a Federal uniform they asked to what command he belonged.

Sam replied, "To Captain Rice's at Fredericktown."

Satisfied, they passed on, swearing vengeance against any Rebels that might fall in their way.

Sam then advised his wife to drive on while he traveled in the brush for a while. He had scarcely left the road when he saw a whole regiment of Federal soldiers not more than half a mile off, coming directly toward his family. Sam, from the woods, could observe their maneuvers. They stopped beside the wagon and talked to his wife for a few minutes. They turned the team of oxen around and took his family along their way.

Noticing this Sam became enraged. Being acquainted with an old

Rebel citizen near this place he decided to go to visit him, for no doubt he would know if any good Rebel soldiers were nearby. Sam was overjoyed upon hearing from this old friend that James Cato and Wash Nabors were taking a nap in the barn while he stood on the lookout. Sam repaired to the barn at once, told them the fate of his family, and asked for their assistance.

After getting something to eat and some provisions to take along, the three of them started through the dense forest until they caught sight of the family at about sundown. Before darkness had set in they had killed a man apiece of the contingent that had made Sam's family turn back. These men lurked around camp all night. About every two hours Cato, Nabors, and Sam would meet at a certain hill and report progress. Sam made a great many random shots, but during the night he must have killed as many as fifteen men. His comrades thought they too had done as well or better. A long time later they learned that they had actually killed thirty while they slithered around in the dark without being followed.

Upon the approach of morning, Sam and his two pals fell back to a high hill until the contingent continued toward Bloomfield. Throughout the day their skirmish lines were so strong that the three bushwhackers could get in only a few shots at long range, especially at their scouts, and during the entire day they were not certain of killing more than two of their men.

The three of them remained hiding in the woods, as near to the troops as possible, until they arrived in the very suburbs of Bloomfield. They they started back along the road in the dark, intending to pick off stragglers.

Sam now had the greatest and most joyful surprise of all, for, sitting by the roadside without oxen and wagon or any provisions or bedding or change of clothing, he found his wife and children. He suddenly remembered a passage of Scripture that his mother had once read aloud to him. It was from the Book of Samuel and gave an account of the Philistines who captured the Ark of the Covenant. They carried it from one place to another, but its presence only meant bad luck — many thousands died. Finally, to get it out of their hands, the Philistines hitched up a yoke of cattle to a cart and, without any driver, sent it out of the country. The Federals, however, instead of following the Philistines to the point of giving her a cart and oxen and presents of gold to get rid of her when so many of their men had been shot during the day, instead confiscated her ox and wagon and left her to starve in an unknown wilderness.

Naturally the family rejoiced at seeing Sam so unexpectedly, but they were starving. Believing that they may have been left there especially to trap him, Sam took up his position about 200 yards away from them while two companions went to get something for them to eat. After their return Sam made a fire for his wife in the woods and gave her directions to follow on the following morning. He told her to reach the home of one of his friends. Then he hurried to that friend immediately, asking him to convey the family to his home. And he did so.

During the evening of that same day, having procured the use of a team, Sam was able to collect them and start toward Arkansas.

Fortunately they were together long before the enemy expected them to be. Colonel McNeal sent out a party from Bloomfield in the hope of overtaking them before they had found each other. The Federal company under Captain Hicks found their trail and followed them to the St. Francis River. But by that time Sam and his family had gotten across. They arrived safely at Captain Bolin's camp. They were soon housed and provided with the necessaries of life, in the charming community where a score of pleasant families were residing.

CHAPTER 13

Now that Sam had succeeded in getting his family to Greene County, Arkansas, he settled on a piece of land whose owner had left for parts unknown. He intended to remain there until the owner should return, which might not be until the end of the war. During the month of April in 1863 he called himself an "honest farmer." By the tenth of May he had completed the planting of a field of corn, and his wife had put in a large vegetable garden.

They were both quite contented. They even started raising chickens and pigs and they had a milk cow also. It was pleasant to realize that the family would be well cared for while he returned to his main business — that of killing his enemies.

The day came when Sam took six men and set out for Castor Creek in Madison County. They intended to track down some notorious scamps who had previously put the Federals on their trail, besides constantly annoying various Southern citizens by reporting their whereabouts to the Federals.

They passed west of Bloomfield, through the Southern part of Madison County. About daylight on the fourth day from home, they secreted their horses and left three men to guard them. Sam and the others proceeded to spy out the men whom they had come to punish. They did not find any of them that first day. After returning to camp in the woods by sunset, they traveled about three miles to the home of an old friend. They counted on having a good night's sleep and some good food for themselves as well as for the horses.

On arriving, their old friend received them pleasantly, but he explained that he was not well and his guests would have to care for their own horses. After supper they tied the horses in a neighboring thicket. Because the weather was stormy they themselves went to an old tobacco barn for shelter. On one side it was about a hundred yards from the woods and on the other about two hundred yards. One man remained on watch the whole time, so the others slept soundly. As none of them had slept for more than an hour in each twenty-four since leaving home, the sentry fell asleep.

In the morning Sam stepped out to take a peep at the weather and was saluted by a shot that struck the board just above his head. He sprang into the barn, raised the alarm, and studied the position of the enemies. He soon discovered that they were about thirty strong, completely surrounding the barn, posted behind the stumps of old trees at a distance of about 150 yards.

Sam noticed that the extent of their circle made their lines very week. Those in front of the barn seemed much the strongest. He ordered his men to remove the underpinning from one place in the rear of the barn. All of them crept through this aperture, lying on the ground and being protected from observation by a pile of rubbish. Taking the lead, Sam directed the men to follow in a straight line but to keep twenty or thirty feet apart.

He started at full speed. Before he had gotten fifty yards the Federals who were in sight of him fired off their guns. Though he was not killed he felt a stringing sensation on the point of his shoulder. That afterwards proved to be a slight abrasion caused by a musket ball. On reaching the line, he shot the two men who were guarding that point, without making the least halt. At the same time he felt a thrill of pity for them and wished that they were alive again and on the side of the Rebels.

Sam's men followed him through to the woods, but one of them was pierced by a musket ball just as he reached the edge of the timber. When they reached the woods they were much relieved because the timber was very thick. They reached their horses although they had been afraid the Federals might have found them. They mounted and rode back to the barn intending to give the Federals a little brush, but they were all gone.

They then made their way around to the friend whose barn they had used during the night, only to discover that the Federals had killed him. They had also committed many other depredations. The kind lady who had thus so unexpectedly become a widow was in the throes of uncontrollable sorrow, but from her broken sentences Sam and his men learned that a citizen by the name of Wammack was with the soldiers and was probably the informant at whose instigation this tragedy had been brought about. She had noticed that, as the soldiers rode in the direction of Fredericktown, Wammack was turning toward his own home.

Sam decided to try to get Wammack at once. He ordered the three men with him to take the horses out of the neighborhood, traveling over ground where they would occasionally make plain tracks. They were to go as far as a certain creek, eight or ten miles off, and then to turn back, riding in the creek for some distance, then concealing themselves in the bushes near the residence of a Mr. Honn.

When the arrangements were made they separated. Sam and two men had not proceeded far, keeping near the road, before they discovered three men coming from the direction of Wammack's house. When they came close Sam hailed them. Leaving their guns behind Sam and his two companions stepped out into the road to inquire the way to Cape Girardeau.

Sam said to them, "We obtained furloughs yesterday at Ironton and are on our way to Illinois to see our families. But a few miles back we met some soldiers who said they'd gotten into a skirmish with bushwhackers and were going to Fredericktown to bring out the whole force. So we thought we'd be wise to hide in the woods until they came back this way."

They took it for granted that these were Federal soldiers, and one of them in a jubilant manner explained that he was with the soldiers at the time. He said they had killed four of the bushwhackers as well as the old Rebel who had harbored them, and that if he'd had his way he'd have burned up the whole premises.

Sam said, "Maybe we'd better go to the main road and wait until the force comes back." But the other objected, saying that he wanted to see who would be burying those dead bushwhackers.

He had been so friendly that Sam by this time thought he could risk asking his name. He said it was Wammack. When he made a motion to proceed Sam and his men drew their revolvers and told him he was a prisoner.

The two men with him had previously given Sam a sign to prove that they were Rebels, so Sam now told them that they could go but requested them to bury the dead at the place where there had been such slaughter so recently. They cheerfully agreed to do so.

Wammack suddenly jerked out his own revolver and, after an attempt to shoot one of Sam's men, broke to run. The movement was so unexpected that he got nearly forty yards away before Sam succeeded in killing him.

Now, feeling free to leave that part of the country, Sam and his men went to Wayne County. While they were having supper there with an old Rebel a young man came in and said, "About five miles from here, on Los Creek, I saw some Federals putting up for the night."

On receiving this pleasant information Sam determined to go and take them "out of the wet," as one of the boys expressed it. After feeding their horses and taking their rations they were soon on the way for that purpose.

They found the place without much difficulty and knocked on the door of the house. The man of the house, in answer to their question, assured them that there were five Federals sleeping in the stable loft above their horses. After telling the old man who they were and ordering him not to leave the house, Sam and his men surrounded the stable which stood in the middle of a lot of perhaps about half an acre. Having taken their positions, Sam set fire to a haystack that stood in the corner of the lot. When the hay blazed up, the light awoke the Federals who sprang to their arms in fright.

Sam hailed them, demanding their surrender, telling them that he was Sam Hildebrand and that with twenty men he had them completely in his clutches.

"But," said Sam, "if you will surrender without firing a gun you'll be let off on easy terms."

To this they agreed and, coming down from the loft, they piled their arms in the lot. Sam then ordered two of his men to extinguish the fire in the haystack that had caught in the fence. Then he negotiated with the prisoners in a friendly and satisfactory manner. Rough jokes were passed back and forth, and they repeated some of the bloody tales that had been circulating in camps about Sam Hildebrand, representing him as a hero more daring and dreadful than Jack the Giant Killer.

At this time there were two of Captain Bolin's men in jail at Ironton. They had been captured while on a scout up Black River in Reynolds County, Missouri. As these prisoners belonged to the command stationed at that place, Sam proposed that they pledge that by some means they would manage to let those two boys escape. In that case they could be released and permitted to retain their personal property. To this they agreed. Sam let them retain their empty pistols, but kept their rifles and horses.

All of these men stayed together through the morning, taking breakfast with the old man who seemed highly pleased at the turn matters had taken. Occasionally he, too, contributed to some of the timely jokes.

After breakfast the Federals made their way on foot, carrying a pass from Sam written by one of his men. This pass would prevent any of the Rebels from molesting them on their way.

After a short consultation with his men, Sam concluded it was time to make their enemies in St. François County pay their taxes to the Southern Confederacy. On the evening of the last day in May they rode into the little town of Big River Mills and made a haul on the story of John B. Highley. Not being certain of his politics they were very light on him. They then rode six miles further on to John Bean's store in Flat River, arriving there at about eleven o'clock in the night. He was known to be a strong Union man and one of his sons belonged to the Big River mob. They generously supplied themselves with such articles as were needed by the families at Captain Bolin's camp.

A few days after Sam's return to Greene County the two boys who had been in prison at Ironton came in and related to Sam that the guards who permitted them to escape had told them about the contract enacted upon the morning the hayfield.

Sam said, "Those Federals deserve credit for keeping their word."

CHAPTER 14

Sam selected seven good men and struck out for Negro-Wool Swamp, on the way visiting Southern friends and passing the time pleasantly with them. They covered but a few miles each day until they neared their destination. The object of this trip was to take in a couple of very noisy Union men, in order to give them a nice necktie manufactured from the textile fabric of nature's own production on the young hickories in the shady woods.

While they were on the lookout for those particular men, a scout of fifteen or twenty Yankees came into the neighborhood. Sam decided to let the two meddlesome Unionists rest for the present and to give the Federals a chase. Having ascertained the exact location of this group, at sundown Sam gave one of them a dead shot from Kill-Devil. That was all that was necessary for a start, and it turned out to be a running start.

Upon seeing the course they took, Sam guessed that they were bound for Bloomfield, so he and his men started in pursuit. It was obvious that the Federals knew who was after them, so they gave no show for a fight. Being much better acquainted with the country than they were, Sam and one of his men followed a nearer route and got in ahead of them while the other boys kept up the chase. When Sam and his partner had gained the point, they came at full speed. As they passed, both fired at the same time. Only one man fell. Because old

Kill-Devil was in the habit of tearing a tolerable large hole there was no doubt of which of them had succeeded. From that point on until within a few miles of Bloomfield the chase was in vain. As Sam said, :A streak of greased lightning could hardly have caught them."

Realizing that a considerable force would now be sent out in the vicinity of Negro-Wool Swamp to clear the country of bushwhackers, Sam concluded not to return to that place but to wind around south of Bloomfield. Suddenly they ran into a man by the name of Crane, for whom one of Captain Bolin's men had been hunting for more than a year. As that particular man was not along, Sam and his men took it upon themselves to shoot Crane. After that they made their way to Wayne County, where they remained for several days, enjoying the luxuries placed at their disposal by friends.

They then took a scout on Black River and stopped with a German who had always professed great friendship for them. On this occasion he greeted them very warmly and seemed to put himself to a great deal of inconvenience to make them comfortable. He stood watch for them while they slept in an unoccupied house. After three or four hours Sam was aroused by the sound of horses' feet. By the time he had awakened his men they were completely surrounded. Through a crack Sam saw their old friend the German on horseback and in line within the Federal soldiers.

At this juncture two of Sam's men were in favor of surrendering, but Sam said, "Follow me!"

There was a dense forest in front of the house, not more than a hundred and fifty yards off. Sam made for it in his fleetest manner, holding his gun in his left hand and his revolver in his right. He wanted to kill the German as he ran but that man was on the opposite side of the house. A whole volley was fired at the Rebels as they ran. One man was killed and two were badly wounded but not sufficiently to disable them. Sam himself received four slight wounds. His own gang fired two or three shots apiece, killing two horses and wounding one man seriously in the face.

On gaining the woods they felt good over their narrow escape. They made their way toward a gap in the bluff about half a mile off, through which they knew the Federals could not easily ride. After gaining that point they stopped to rest and reloaded. Then they made their way to the top of the bluff and discovered through the thick brush, at a distance of not more than 200 yards, the Federals approaching slowly and cautiously.

Sam commanded, "Fire in the same order in which you are lying, so that no two men fire at the same Federal."

When they were fairly within gun shot Sam gave the word, and all his men fired. Four of the Federals fell dead and one, badly wounded, broke down the hill calling loudly on the name of the Lord.

Sam's men quickly reloaded, and they followed cautiously in the direction of the German's house where they had come so near to being taken in. On gaining the edge of the woods they discovered the Federals sitting on their horses close to the house. The one of them who wore shoulder straps appeared to be making a speech. The distance being about 150 yards, some of Sam's men objected to shooting, but Sam gave the word slowly "— Ready — aim — fire!" At the discharge of all those rifles four of the Federals fell, and the gentleman with shoulder straps was helped from his horse.

At this juncture the remaining Federals began to form into about twenty different lines, with only one abreast, each man being in advance, and each one bringing up his rear. It was a novel military position but it worked well, and in almost an instant they seemed to be spirited away. No more was seen of them.

Sam and his men made their way down Black River for about two miles and camped for the night. The next morning at sunrise Sam went calling on a friend who lived back in the woods, to obtain provisions for his men. The friend told him that the Federals had left for Greenville immediately after the second round against them. They had given orders to some citizens to bury their dead and on the following day to send the horses to Patterson. These horses included those they had captured from Sam's party.

After Sam had procured the provisions he needed he hastened back to camp with the news. After eating they hurried over to the Patterson Road, selected a good position, and waited impatiently for the men to come along with the horses. At ten o'clock that morning an old man about sixty years of age and three little boys came slowly along. After they had come sufficiently near, Sam stepped out and addressed the old man in a friendly manner, stating his business. At this the old man made some objections as he removed his old cobpipe.

"Well, it's against my orders to deliver the horses up to Sam Hildebrand."

At that he relinquished the horses, and Sam saw his smile of secret satisfaction. The little boys, however, were badly scared, seeming to understand what was happening. Sam took possession of the fourteen horses. According to previous arrangements, five of Sam's men struck out for Greene County with them, while one of them remained with Sam, on foot, for the purpose of killing the German who had betrayed them. Actually his action had caused one of the bravest men in the Confederacy to be killed.

After sending the old man and the little boys away, Sam took leave of his men. Then he and his one comrade repaired to a neighboring hill and rested and slept by turns until sunset.

From the position they occupied Sam had a fair view of the surrounding country and particularly of the main road leading to Patterson. During the day all was quiet, save when a citizen occasionally passed along the road.

As night approached Sam and his partner became restless. Before the sun had shed its last rays upon the neighboring hills they were on the way to the scene of yesterday's tragedy. It was not yet entirely dark, so they took up a position in the fence corner near the house. There they lay in silent impatience until the gray horizon warned that the watch for the present was ended. Quietly they retired to the house of a friend for breakfast, which was very welcome because they had eaten nothing except a piece of cornbread since the preceding morning.

Sam and his pal then proceeded to the house of their German enemy, having sworn in wrath to take his life before leaving this part of the country. They succeeded in gaining a position within 100 yards of his house and directly in front of the door. Here they remained all day. At about four o'clock that afternoon two strange men rode up to the house and held a conversation with the lady of the house for several minutes at the door. They then rode off in the direction that they had come from. It was evident that the German had left with the Federals the day before during their retreat and that he had made no arrangements for a long absence. It was more than probable that those two men had come to see whether or not the way was clear.

Sam and his friend felt that their expectation would soon be realized, but they were impatient. After dark they changed their position to a place in the fence corner, near the woodpile, and there they remained until the night was half spent. Finally they were made glad by the sound of horses' feet coming from the direction of Patterson. They could perceive that the noise was made by only one horse.

Advancing slowly, the German approached the house, alighted at the woodpile, and tied his horse to the end of one of the limbs within a few feet of Sam. Just then Sam and his pal arose and demanded his surrender.

The old fellow was badly alarmed and called alternately upon the Almighty and Mr. Hildebrand for mercy.

Sam told him, "It is useless for you to beg for mercy. You are our prisoner, and we expect to take you to headquarters as a prisoner of war."

His wife came out to the fence immediately on his arrival, and it was her presence alone that prevented Sam from shooting her husband at once. Sam held the gun at him while his comrade went to the stable to secure another horse. Finding nothing there but an old mule he came back leading it with a bridle. Sam asked the lady to lend him a saddle, and in a few minutes she came back with her own side saddle, explaining that it was the only saddle on the place.

Sam said, "I would not rob a lady, so keep the saddle. I am sorry from my heart to be compelled to cause you any trouble. War has no mercy, and through it all I hope that you will be protected from harm."

Sam tied the German's hands behind him, then tied him to the mule without any saddle. The mule humped up his back and gave a specimen of mule melody on a base note that re-echoed among the hills. They started leading the horse and the mule, but they had to stop several times to let the mule finish his braying, for each time he refused to budge an inch while he was in the midst of his complaints.

They traveled about a mile and then set about hanging the German. He spoke only once and then the mule chimed in. Before he had finished the German was hanging from a limb. To render his duplicity even more apparent, it should be borne in mind that he was now wearing a Federal uniform. Perhaps he had enlisted during this very day.

Previous to hanging him Sam had removed his pocket book and a revolver.

Mounting the horse and the mule, the two of them went on about two miles then stopped at the house of a friend and asked for something to eat. That friend, on hearing what had just taken place, pleaded manfully for the lady whom they had recently widowed.

He said, "She is a good woman, and she has done many a good deed. Now she will be entirely dependent on the charity of the community for support. Do please give the horse and the mule back to her."

Sam readily consented to this and added, "Please give her the pocketbook also, for I've found that it contains forty dollars."

The danger was that anyone delivering the horse and mule and pocketbook to her would be considered implicated. It was therefore agreed that the friend should return these while it was yet night. He could throw the pocketbook over the fence into the yard.

After this was agreed upon Sam and his companion started on foot toward their Arkansas homes and arrived there safely.

CHAPTER 15

Sam remained at home for two weeks plowing, and then he went scouting in the vicinity of Mingo Swamp with eight men. They watched around for several days with the intention of capturing some of the famous scamps who had been giving trouble to the Rebels ever since the beginning of the war. Being too cowardly to enlist in the army they were staying at home and constantly annoying peaceable citizens by making false reports against them.

Having failed to get any of them at this try, Sam and his company made another trip over into Castor Creek, for they were always eager to go to parts of the country frequented by the Federals. They had been on Castor Creek one day and night when a party of Federals came along, camping within a short distance of Bollinger's mill. Sam and his company were quietly enjoying themselves in the nook of a rocky range of brushy hills when a runner came to inform them of the new arrivals. He was not able to report the exact number of the Federals who had arrived.

It was with difficulty that Sam restrained his men to wait until the proper hour of the night to attack, but at ten o'clock he gave the word to set out. Going around the hills they struck the main road after about a mile. They rode very slowly until they routed the pickets, then dashed on and crowded them into camp. But they had not received information about the true position of the camp quarters. Consequently, they met with difficulty.

The Federals had chosen a narrow place in the road and had turned their wagons across it. It was Sam's custom to dash through an enemy camp, but on this occasion he was suddenly stopped. The Federals opened up heavy fire, killing two of the invaders and slightly wounding another before they had time to retreat. Afterwards they learned that they had wounded three of the Federals, one of whom died the next morning. Sam's crowd had made a mistake that they regretted, and at first they wanted only to return to Greene County, Arkansas, where they could take care of their wounded companions.

Sam consented and then started off alone toward St. François County in Missouri. This seemed like a good chance to take vengeance against R. M. Cole for what he had done at the time Sam's brother Frank was hung by the Big River mob. Sam still had conflicting impressions concerning Cole's guilt. Certainly Cole was a Southerner, and it had been his duty as a civil officer to wrest Frank from the clutches of the merciless mob. Later, it is true, Sam learned that Cole was innocent, but at the time he had a different opinion.

Carefully he avoided the hundreds of soldiers whose duty it was to catch him. Unobserved by anyone who would be likely to inform against him, Sam reached Cole's farm on Flat River and discovered that he had not yet finished plowing. He went around to the back of the farm and hitched his horse Charley to a sapling in the woods. Then, taking Kill-Devil in hand, he cautiously approached the cornfield where the plow had been left. At sunset he hid in a fence corner about ten rows from where Cole had plowed the last furrow. It was now after dark, and Sam was satisfied that Cole had stopped plowing for the night.

Sam went back to where he had hitched his horse, unsaddled him and went in search of feed. There was an abundance of oats already cut in the field. On the way back he crossed a melon patch and made a splendid supper of ripe melons, feeling very thankful for such good luck. Now he had only to wait for morning, and he made himself as comfortable as possible.

In the morning once again he took his station in the fence corner with old Kill-Devil cocked. It seemed a long delay before Cole made his appearance, following along behind the plow and singing merrily. His merry mood had a strange effect upon Sam who felt a strange weakness coming over him. He was unable to fire. He decided at first to let him plow one more round, and he chuckled to himself as Cole walked deliberately away as if nothing was about to go wrong with him.

When Cole came around again, as merrily as before, Sam raised old Kill-Devil to his face and was in the act of pulling the trigger when he heard a stick crack in the woods. This and some other imaginary noises caused him to delay until Cole was too far off — so a good chance was lost. Sam was by this time becoming nervous. He bit his fingers in what hunters call the "buck ague," and the more he thought about killing Cole the more nervous he got. He had never felt that way before, and it struck him that perhaps he was not engaged in a just cause. There might be something wrong in this matter after all.

Of course he knew that it would never do for him to remain squatting in that fence corner any longer. He would either have to shoot or leave. He asked himself, "Can it be possible that he is innocent of the charge brought against him by my friends? Have my suspicions been groundless?"

Sam began to think of letting Cole live, but having ridden several hundred miles especially for the purpose of killing him and then going back home without having done it seemed very foolish indeed.

All this time Sam was sitting quietly. Once he almost rose and left, but just then Cole was making his third round and was too close. Sam did raise his gun and took a bead on him to make his decision while the man was completely in his power. Then definitely "Live on, sir! Live on!" was the decision. As soon as Cole turned away Sam hastily left for fear of being tempted again. As soon as he could safely do so he mounted his horse and rode away. Never before in his life had he felt so happy, for he was now sure that never should Cole be hurt by his hand.

On his homeward trip Sam stopped in the vicinity of Bloomfield which he knew was in the hands of the Federals. He wanted to pay his respects to Captain Hicks, commander of the company which had followed Sam's family to the St. Francis River and boasted that he was the man who had shot Sam at the Flat Woods. Sam had never bothered to deny that tale, but he wanted to govern himself as though it might be true.

Sam lay around Captain Hicks' residence for four days and nights, getting provisions from his smoke house each morning before he made his appearance. On the evening of the fourth day Hicks rode up to his house and a few minutes later walked into the garden with his wife. Sam walked up to the garden fence and spoke to him. Hicks showed how agitated he felt and started toward his house.

Sam raised his gun and said, "Come over here, for I want to have a little talk with you."

With some reluctance he did walk toward Sam, asking, "Who are you?"

Sam replied, "I am Sam Hildebrand. I understand you have been hunting for me for some time. I decided to come and find out what you wanted."

Suddenly Hicks made a lick at Sam with a hoe which he had been holding in his hand. Immediately Sam ended his existence by shooting him. After that he effected his escape to Arkansas.

CHAPTER 16

At about the middle of August, 1863, two brave boys who had assisted Sam on several of his trips to St. François County asked for his assistance in return. He agreed and started toward a place called Hamburg with fifteen men under his command. The intention was to take three or four Dutchmen who had given the relatives of these two young men a great deal of trouble. They had caused those relatives to be robbed and some of them to be imprisoned.

This day Sam's contingent crossed into Butler County and then into Stoddard. Passing south and east of Bloomfield, they crossed Little River above Buffington and entered Scott County. All their traveling was by night, and they created no disturbance until they reached the point toward which they were aiming. Then, at about ten o'clock in the forenoon, they surrounded the house of one of the guilty men. Recognizing them as Union soldiers he came out without waiting to be called.

He commenced by addressing them in Dutch, and Sam told him that they did not understand that language.

Then the Dutchman began to talk in broken English as he advanced. He was in the act of extending his hand toward the man nearest to him when he suddenly realized his mistake. He then called to his wife, and the whole family crowded out of the house, placing themselves near Sam and imploring Sam's men in broken English to spare their father.

At the bottom of his heart Sam cursed the man who had first invented war. Still, war on one side and mercy on the other would lead only to death. Therefore he marched the Dutchman off about a mile and hung him to a leaning tree.

About an hour later they approached the house of another one of those cunning informers. He broke out at the back door and ran so fast that they had to fire before he could be brought down.

After this Sam and his gang pushed on to get a couple more who lived at Hamburg. On entering that place they met a volley of musket shots that made their ears ring. One of Sam's men was killed on the spot. Thereupon they charged the enemy although they numbered about twelve. They took refuge behind a dilapidated old frame house. Sam placed some of his men in positions to command both ends of the building, while others marched up to the front of the house and set it on fire.

By this time the shooting had attracted the attention of Federals in the vicinity. They came to the rescue of their friends, and before Sam was aware of their presence they had surrounded him and the other attackers. Four of Sam's men were wounded but none killed when they made a dash to clear the lines.

Sam began to think he and his men had met more than they could match because, as they retreated, the enemy followed in a solid phalanx. Sam's horses were put to the utmost of their speed, his wounded were left behind, and the chase was gloriously exciting. After they had gone about two miles they felt that they had gained a bit, but they were not allowed to breathe deeply until they had gained the Little River and had swum across to Coon Island. They had lost nearly everything they had except their horses, and they were badly injured. Some of Sam's men had lost their guns, and others had lost every bit of fight they'd ever had in them.

The Federals made no attempt to cross the river, but Sam had to view the matter as a definite defeat. One of his men had been killed and four wounded, prisoners no doubt who would be shot. Later it turned out that those four were retained and treated well as prisoners of war and were actually exchanged within three months and returned to the Greene County Confederacy. After that Sam felt respect for General Steele.

The day of the defeat they left Coon Island and struck the St. Francis River at Twelve Mile Creek. There they remained several days recruiting their horses. In the meantime Sam went on foot to Flat

William Clarke Quantrill, the guerrilla chief. Sam fought, on occasion alongside of Quantrill.

Carl Breihan Collection

Woods to pay his respects to George F. Oller who had long been spending most of his time watching for a chance to defeat Sam Hildebrand. Aside from his boisterous threats he had the habit of marking out "Old Sam" on trees and shooting that figure at various distances. Of course his vindictive spirit was not manifested against one man alone but against all the Southern sympathizers. At one time he had gone to the St. Francis River where some Southern boys were in the habit of bathing. Near the high rock from which they were fond of plunging he drove some sharp cedar stakes which he placed just under the surface of the water. Fortunately when the boys next went there to bathe the water had fallen a few inches, exposing the ends of the stakes. Therefore the boys discovered them before making the leap. Of course Oller had done all this from the patriotic motive of subjugating the South.

On arriving in the neighborhood Sam learned from a kind German lady who mistook him for a Federal that the hunt for Sam Hildebrand was still going on. He learned also that Oller's real zeal for the good of the Union cause was not abated by his failure ever to hit the figure he had been calling "Old Sam" on the large oak near his house, nor by his failure to kill the innocent children that he expected to become Rebels at some future time.

That night Sam inspected Oller's premises, and before daylight he had taken his position. During the whole day Oller did not make his appearance. When night came Sam repaired to the house of a friend and secured two days' rations, then returned to his ambush, and slept until the peep of day, but for another whole day he was disappointed. On the third day, late in the evening, Oller did make his appearance.

He walked slowly toward his house with a gun on his shoulder. On reaching the pig pen he climbed over the fence and marked a pig.

Sam shot him through and hastily left the place. On gaining the top of a small hill a few hundred yards off he could hear the pig squealing. Mr. Oller had fallen across it, and it was not able to extricate itself.

On returning to where his men were resting Sam selected five of them who were more than willing to continue with him and permitted the rest to return to Arkansas. As soon as it was dark he and his five followers started for Irondale on the St. Louis and Iron Mountain Railroad. Just after dark in the early part of September they entered that town and saw no soldiers or any citizens at all on the streets except Dr. Poston. They compelled him to knock at Bean's store and ask to be admitted. All of them entered without any trouble. They took all the goods they could conveniently pack and then returned to Arkansas by way of Black River.

CHAPTER 17

Sam felt under obligation to help some of the boys on a trip to the neighborhood from which they had been driven. About the middle of September, after having rested for about a week, he set out with six men from Springfield, Missouri, to make a raid in the vicinity of that city. Sam, being a stranger in that area, had little to say in programming that particular raid. They started without purse or scrip, intending to rely altogether on their good luck for supplies.

From Greene County, Arkansas, they traveled through Randolph and entered Missouri in Ripley County, then had to delay because one of the men had lost a horse. They were in a place known as the Irish Wilderness, where they planned to rest a day and hunt. The evening before they struck camp they were joined by a young man in civilian clothes who claimed to be on his way to enlist with the Rebel army. Saying that he was on his way to Arkansas he asked permission to stop with them over night. Nobody made any objection.

After the general confusion of striking camp, making fires, attending to the horses, and so forth, this new companion began asking a series of questions regarding the part of the country through which they had been operating since the beginning of the war. After answering some of his questions about the land, Sam's men started relating to him some of the thrilling incidents that had filled their days. He was a keen listener, and at the amusing stories he laughed heartily. After hearing of many dangerous feaats and bloody deeds, he began his own narrative of harbreadth escapes and heroic adventures, especially in Kentucky.

They had scarcely noticed the change from twilight to darkness, so much were they entertained by the new companion's pleasant stories. All of them had agreed to spend the following day in an oldfashioned deer hunt among the wild hills surrounding. At morning one word loudly spoken was enough to bring the whole squad to a half-recumbent position. Suddenly the attention of each one turned to the spot where the new comrade had deposited himself for sleep a few hours earlier. He was gone. But this was not all. One of the best horses was gone too. The men cared little about the loss of the horse because they had plenty of experience in "raising horses," but it was clear that they had been gulled by a young adventurist Union loyalist. Besides, they now had to consider themselves "shark proof." And of course there was no reason to believe that the misfortune would end there. The "sharper" had succeeded in getting their plans for the trip ahead of them.

During the preparation of the morning meal the subject of their misfortune was freely discussed. Who was their deceiver? What could he do with the information he had obtained from them? A majority were in favor of continuing according to plan, but one man joined Sam in opposing any further movement in the direction of Springfield. However, it was not Sam's trip and therefore he did not feel at liberty to say much about it. He did feel his trust of that unfortunate incident would haunt him to the grave, but he could not convince the others and finally submitted cheerfully to going along with the majority.

Sam and two others rode over to the edge of the settlement to get a horse and succeeded in finding one. The owner was a noted Rebel, so they had to pass themselves off as Union soldiers. In this way they obtained the horse without any difficulty. On the way back to the camp Sam saw some deer on the side of an adjoining hill. Fearing that the boys in camp may have failed to kill meat for supper, he selected a nice buck and shot him on the spot.

They dressed the meat preparatory to carrying it into camp and then built a fire to broil some of it for dinner. Squatted around the fire they suddenly heard a boisterous command: "Surrender!" They sprang to their feet, revolvers in hand, and they found themselves confronted by five of Captain Bolin's men. They had left Greene County several days ahead of Sam's crowd and had been visiting the man from whom they had taken the horse. In quick recognition a general congratulation was the only military demonstration between them.

These five "bushwhackers" had been concealed near the house of the Old Rebel from whom they had taken the horse and they had considered the men with Sam as Federals. Captain Bolin's men had been alerted and tracked them to the Irish Wilderness. The horse was returned to the rightful owner, and another horse was obtained in the same neighborhood the following night.

While the venison was broiling there was prolonged discussion of the "sharper" who had gotten away with one of the horses. Captain Bolin's company was able to explain that the adventurous Yankee detective had been in that neighborhood for a week or two, repeating the same story, but evidently he had now left the environs. At any rate he was not seen again.

The following morning Sam's whole party set out for Springfield, and that evening they reached the vicinity of Thomasville in Oregon County. They were warned not to travel in the daytime if they wanted to avoid a fight, and the fact was that all they wanted to do was to enable some of the boys to avenge certain wrongs they had received at the hands of certain Union men in Missouri. They made a heavy draw on some of their Rebel friends for provisions and horse-feed, and then they resumed the journey.

The following morning they were quartered in the woods near a small town in Howell County called Lost Camp. And old friend who lived nearby brought them two or three bottles of "burst-head," and that had the effect of making some of the boys believe they had just fought a great battle — that the United States Government had taken refuge in a deep cavern stopped by a big rock upon which they were dancing.

That night they resumed the journey and by morning they were in a beautiful little town called Vera Cruz in Douglas County. The following night they had arrived at Panther Creek in Webster County, and one of the boys was disappointed because a supposedly good friend refused to give him the supplies he requested. During the forenoon they were surprised by a party of about sixty Federal soldiers. Before they were aware, the Federals charged upon them, yelling and shooting at a furious rate. Sam instantly realized that any attempt at resistance would be folly, so he yelled at the boys to run. There was no time for them to mount their horses, so they had to depend on their feet. Through the dense forest they had the advantage of their enemies. Sam and four of his men kept together for about a mile and then they took up a position on a high hill and remained there until late in the evening.

Finally they saw one of their own men cautiously emerging from a dense thicket in the valley at the foot of the hill. Sam made his way down the hill within a hundred yards of him and then called him by name. Even then it was some time before he recognized Sam. Fortunately he was well acquainted with that part of the country where they would have to pass in making their way back to Arkansas. At daybreak they started on what they realized would be a perilous journey of two hundred miles on foot without blankets or provisions — with only pistols and one rifle, for Sam had managed to escape with old Kill-Devil in hand.

The following morning they ran into a herd of sheep and succeeded in catching one. They then made their way down into a deep ravine where they were not likely to be discovered. They built a fire and fared sumptuously.

The next day they managed to kill a deer to sustain them. On the following night they reached a good friend near Vera Cruz where they met another one of their boys. He was no better posted as to the fate of the company than Sam was. After many privations they did get back to Arkansas and, fortunately for Sam, as he said, he never again received an invitation to take a trip to Springfield under the command of an inexperienced leatherhead.

About a week after return to camp another one of the contingent managed to come in, looking somewhat subjugated. It was afterward learned that two of their men had been killed at the time of the routing and that the others were taken prisoner. None of them ever returned during the war.

CHAPTER 18

Having selected four good men, Sam started on another trip to St. François County, Missouri, on the 10th of November. They traveled at night only and arrived in the vicinity of Fredericktown about midnight. They stopped at the home of a well known friend who was surprised to see them. The cry of "Hildebrand" had been raised in the whole community during the past ten days. The Federals, with the assistance of various citizens, had been scouring the woods between there and Farmington.

Such a report during the last ten days could only work favorably for Sam, for a second search in such a short time was not likely. They went to a dense thicket near the residence of a Mr. North. Being very tired they lay down and slept soundly until the morning sun was looking down upon them. Their old friend had supplied them with two days' rations and some shelled corn for the horses, so they expected to take a good rest.

Suddenly they were startled by the sound of a gun nearby, evidently discharged at them. They had been spied out, their horses tracked, and the thicket surrounded. At a bound, Sam leaped into his saddle and was soon out of the thicket in an opposite direction from where the gun had sounded. On reaching open ground he saw that the Federals were trying to complete a circle around the hill. When they fired at Sam the distance was too great and he remained unhurt. His men had not taken the time to mount, but as they followed him on foot one of them received a bruise on his back from a spent ball. All of them had escaped with no damage except the loss of four horses.

The Federals followed them for about a mile, but they got far enough ahead to give them the dodge by turning at right angles into the St. Francis River bottom. They then made their way back to within a mile of Fredericktown, where they remained for the rest of the day. When night arrived they went in pursuit of their pursuers and found them camped in a lane about six miles northwest of Fredericktown.

Their object now was to get horses. They made their way on foot but found that the end of the lane was guarded. When they went around to the other end they found that too guarded. The horses were within the circle tied to one of the fences. Sam led his men around through the field. Laying down the outside fence very carefully they approached the lane fence on the opposite side from where the horses were tied. Although the night was dark they could distinctly see a sentry slowly walking his beat of about fifty yards, and the stealthy men with Sam were at the end of the beat. When the sentry's back was turned Sam laid the fence down easily. He and his men sprang to a horse apiece, cut the halters, mounted, and were off at full speed before the sentry turned at the other end of his beat.

Of course the hasty flight of Sam and his men caused an alarm in the camp, but they saw no more of the Federals that night. As it was easy to suppose, the Federals spent several days hunting them. For that reason Sam led his men to take up quarters in a place least expected: within a mile of Fredericktown on a certain eminence reached after circling the side of a hill.

On the following day they slept by turns. Sam killed a pig with his knife near the house of a farmer and cooked it in a deep ravine where the fire could not be observed. They had already stolen a sufficiency of feed for their horses. At about ten o'clock that night Sam managed to get a supply of ammunition in Fredericktown by means of a friend. Then they moved seven or eight miles in the direction of Pilot Knob, supplying themselves with horse-feed and provisions for themselves.

At the approach of the next morning, Sam left his men in charge of the horses and instructed them where to meet him in case of any trouble. He went to the gravel road for the purpose of killing a Federal or two. He concealed himself near the road. At about ten o'clock two of them came along and Sam let off his old Kill-Devil at one of them. They wheeled and started back in the direction of Pilot Knob. The one who had been hit was badly wounded and bled freely.

An hour afterwards a squad of perhaps ten soldiers came from the direction of Fredericktown. Wondering whether he should take a shot at them, a feeling of revenge made the decision for Sam. He fired, and one fell. At this the others put their horses at full speed. Soon after they were out of sight another came along in a great hurry as if he meant to overtake the others. On coming up to the dead man in the road he made a momentary stop, of which Sam took the advantage and shot him through.

It now seemed that he had done enough for one day, or at least enough to cause some excitement among the Federals, so he returned to his men and all of them moved about twelve miles in the direction of Farmington. They settled near the St. Francis River on a high bluff that would afford advantages in the event of a fight. It turned out that they were compelled to remain there for several days.

The man in Sam's contingent who had received a bruise on the spine by this time had become so disabled that he could not ride. Reports of the two men who had been killed on the gravel road had created a stir, and Sam's men were the object of a zealous search. The forces had been called out at Pilot Knob, at Fredericktown, and at Farmington. A large number of citizens were searching in earnest. Squads frequently passed in sight of the spot where Sam and his men were settled — often within easy gunshot — but none of them ascended the high bluff.

On the evening of the third day their provisions and horse-feed gave out, and each night Sam went out in search of more. Obtaining feed for the horses was an easy matter, but getting provisions for themselves was not only difficult but dangerous. Sam knew very few people in that section, and on his approach of their houses he invariably found their well-known signal of danger — a towel hung on a nail outside the door. He could easily have killed a hog or a sheep, but he could not run the risk of building a fire to cook it. After their provisions gave entirely out they were twenty-four hours without food. During the second night Sam found some bacon in somebody's smoke house — knowing not whether he was friend or foe and caring still less, he took two hams to camp and his men ate them raw.

On the sixth night he disabled comrade was again well enough to ride. So they moved about fifteen miles, stopping south of Fredericktown. There a friend supplied them with the necessaries, even brought food to their camp cooked and ready for eating. The wounded companion, although able to ride, could never have taken part in a raid, so Sam released him to return to Arkansas alone. All the other men started on a trip to St. François County.

While living at Flat Woods Sam had become acquainted with a man named John Fowler. He professed to be a strong man for the South. Having confidence in his veracity, Sam had entrusted him with plans that he withheld from the others of his neighbors. However, at the time Sam was run off from there by the Federals, Fowler joined the Union army. On learning of this Sam naturally felt mortified, exclaiming, "He betrayed me!" Nevertheless Fowler later sent Sam word not to doubt him. Just the same, his duplicity was so apparent that Sam was determined to kill him at sight. This seemed to be possible because Fowler often came into the neighborhood along with other soldiers. On every one of those occasions he stopped to talk in a friendly manner with Sam's wife, but Sam still regarded him as a spy.

Now as Sam was traveling along with his men after the long siege at the top of the bluff, he ran suddenly upon Fowler about five miles southwest of Fredericktown. They met in a narrow path, and before he hardly had time to recognize Sam, Sam had shot and killed him. It turned out to be an action that Sam would forever afterward regret, for it was later learned that Fowler had left the Federals and at the time was on his way south to join the "bushwhacking department" of the Southern army.

After passing Fredericktown during the night, Sam and his men learned that several companies of the Federals, Home Guards, and Militia, were hunting for Hildebrand in every direction. In fact Sam and his men did come near to being discovered by several squads during the night.

They were hastening on into St. François County, Tom Haile and Sam leading the way. They arrived in Farmington without firing a gun long before the other men caught up with them. The streets were full of people, but they only had time to take a second look when the place seemed to be deserted. Not a man, woman, or child could be found. At this Tom laughed heartily and remarked, "I guess cellar rent must be high in this place."

When the other men caught up Tom told them, "We have found a beautiful town not claimed by anybody, just laying around loose. I'm sorry we can't take it along with us until we find an owner."

After going into a grocery where they had to help themselves they took a hearty drink of some good old liquor, then mounted and rode away. They went on to Big River to look after their former enemies, but none of them was available.

Sam later said, "In our business of killing enemies we met with success everywhere but on Big River. A majority of the miscreants whose hands were dripping with the blood of my brothers are yet permitted to live."

It is true that during this particular ride, for several days and nights, they watched around the houses of the old enemies but to no purpose. It was impossible to find them. It was reported that they were all away from home except Franklin Murphy. Tom Haile was determined that Sam should not kill that man. Tom had exacted a promise from Sam long ago that he never would molest Franklin Murphy or his property. Haile was a man who wielded an influence upon anyone he contacted. He was always in a perfect humor, and the clouds of adversity never seemed to throw a shadow on his brow.

Sam agreed that so far as killing his old enemies was concerned his current trip was a failure. He was now in need of a good horse, and Tom Haile agreed that he ought to demand a good horse, bridle, and saddle, from G. W. Murphy, a man whose nature it was to be quiet and inoffensive and who had strictly attended to his own business during all the struggle. Because he was abundantly able to assist, he ought to contribute that much toward the Southern cause. He and Sam had been raised together, so he complied when Sam made the request. They also took a horse from Orville McIlvaine who lived on the place known as the Baker farm. Sam had been worried about seeing him because he was well known for never parting with a greenback after it got into his safe, but his retiring nature prompted him to conceal himself in the garret until Sam and his men departed.

Now the whole contingent started back home by way of Mingo Swamp, warned by friends that the Federals were thick in that locality. About midnight they arrived at the house of old Bill Coots who had until then always represented himself as a Rebel of unusual bitterness. This time he told Sam that there were no Feds in the neighborhood, neither had there been any for more than a month. He also declared that the men Sam wanted to find were then at home. Sam felt gratified on hearing news so favorable to the success of his enterprise. He asked old Bill Coots to supply the gang with a few days' rations and feed for the horses while they camped at a certain point not more than half a mile distant.

Coots readily consented and invited them to have breakfast with him at sun up. To this they agreed. At their arrival he received them with what was called "Arkansas courtesy." They had gone through such a scanty fattening process while on the St. Francis bluff that the odor from the kitchen of coffee, ham, and eggs made them forget all other considerations for the moment. When they were about to seat themselves at the table old Coots said, "Here, gentlemen — lay your arms on the bed."

But that was not their custom. They seated themselves at the table with them on. They were perhaps half done eating when a ragged-looking Federal stepped up to the door.

In an exulting tone he said, "Well, Coots! You got them, did you?" Then he bawled out, "Surrender!"

At this Sam leaped to his feet and drew his revolver and shot Coots. He then seized his gun which he had left near the door and he cleared the door by about fifteen feet. He shot the Federal with his revolver which he was still holding in his right hand. In a few bounds he had gained the woods unhurt save for a slight wound on the back of his head.

As Sam's men attempted to follow without their guns, two of them were killed, while the remaining one (Tom Haile) soon caught up with Sam, and they made their way to their horses. Fortunately the Federals had not found the horses.

Sam and Tom tarried in the hope that their comrades might catch up with them. When they did not appear Sam was afraid they had been slain. So Sam and Tom mounted their own horses and led the others, making their way to a cane brake about a mile off. From there they sent a citizen back to ascertain the state of affairs. This friend took an old bridle in his hand and made his way over, inquiring of each person he met for a gray mare and a black colt.

On passing the house of old Coots he was halted, but he put on an act of not being the least alarmed. He expressed surprise when he heard about the whole tragedy. The worst of it was that two of Sam's men were killed and lying in front of the house. Upon receiving this news Sam and Tom started home to get a force sufficient to come back and punish the Federals.

CHAPTER 19

On the 15th of December, 1863, Sam started back to Mingo Swamp with ten men. They met with obstacles after their swim in the St. Francis River, but when they reached the neighborhood of the unfortunate tragedy of their previous trip they learned that the Federals had left for Bloomfield the day after the skirmish at old Bill Coots' house. Some of the men they had been expecting to encounter had enlisted in the regular army.

Sam led the way to Mrs. Coots' home for the purpose of seeing the graves of his two brave boys killed after that fatal breakfast. Mrs. Coots confessed that her deceased husband had laid plans for his capture, that the Federals had been camped only a mile away at the time. After Sam had consented to accept the invitation to breakfast the Federals had been notified.

Then Sam and his followers made their way over to Castor Creek to see a friend who, since the beginning of the war, had acted as an agent for the Southerners, receiving and forwarding supplies and medicines. This time they accepted the medicine that had been sent from Farmington, St. François County, Missouri, and started back for Mingo Swamp. The monotony of their journey was relieved by a sight of a Federal approaching. He was apparently riding cautiously, as the road took him down into a small ravine. Being certain he had not noticed them, they left the road and waited for him to appear. When they halted him he seemed very much frightened, but he surrendered quietly.

He explained that he had been to Cairo, Illinois, to see his family and was now on the way back to his command at Fredericktown. He gave such a good account of himself that Sam's men only disarmed him and took his greenbacks which amounted to twelve dollars.

The following night they heard of three more Rebel boys in the neighborhood and sent for them. They agreed to try a trip with Sam's group, so they all left the collected drugs with a friend and returned to Castor Creek to wait for the Federals who might be passing thereon the way between Fredericktown and Cape Girardeau. After they had been there one night and day they hard of two companies of Federals commanded by Captains Cawhorn and Rhoder on their way. After dark Sam and his men proceeded to spy out their exact locality and study the surroundings. It turned out that their position and numbers made it unsafe to charge through the enemy camp as was their custom. Therefore they concluded to bushwhack the Federals. During that night they killed and wounded twelve, and wounded several others according to later information.

At daylight Sam's company went about two miles into a dense thicket with their horses. They put out spies and waited impatiently for the Federals to move. Instead of marching, however, they were charging around public places in the vicinity, threatening Southern sympathizers with annihilation. That day there was no chance to bushwhack them.

A squad of them went to the residence of Dick Cowan, one of Sam's men, burned his house and other buildings and attempted an outrage on one of his sisters. For several days the people in the neighborhood were compelled to suffer glaring insults and wrongs. Each night Sam's men renewed the attack and did some killing. The Federals endured this mode of warfare for several days and nights. However, early on the morning of the seventh day they set out for Cape Girardeau. During their march the Rebels stationed themselves at convenient places. As the Feds came riding along, a deadly fire was poured into their ranks, while their tormentors retreated into the woods. Although this was supposed to encourage them to follow, it only seemed to hurry their march. They were attacked three times before they reached Cape Girardeau.

By this time, Sam's men were anxious to see their families so they started back to Arkansas, taking along the drugs they had cached with a friend. They soon met twenty-eight of Captain Reed's men, who invited them to go with them to Wayne County and perhaps as far north as Iron County. To this Sam consented, but he detailed two of the men to carry the medicines to Arkansas.

Starting on the way they marched in daytime and passed about twenty miles south of Bloomfield and on to Greenville in Wayne County. They arrived about sunset but did not find any Federal troops there to protect its loyalty. They heard of a company of Federals on Lost Creek under Captain Leeper. Taking their informant for a guide, they marched over at once to give them a fight.

Reaching there at about sunrise the next morning they charged into the camp, running their pickets in at full speed. After fighting for only a few minutes those who had not escaped into the brush surrendered. In the fight the Southerners had lost four men killed and six wounded, and fortunately the wounded soon recovered. Of the enemy fifteen had been killed, with eight wounded and ten taken as prisoners. The booty consisted for forty-four rifles, sixty pistols, forty horses, and four hundred dollars in greenbacks, as well as other articles of value to the Rebels or their families.

There was a discussion about what to do with the prioners, and a vote was taken as to whether they should be killed or let loose. In consideration of the wrongs Sam's family had received at their hands and of their well known cruelty, he made a speech in favor of killing them. When the whole vote was counted Sam found himself in the minority by just two votes. Therefore the prisoners were released unarmed and on foot.

Later it was learned that during the previous evening they had killed an old man by the name of Tom McKee and burned his house with other buildings on the premises. If this outrage had been known before that vote, no doubt they would have been shot. On being informed of the fact Sam's company sent a scout after them, but they had left the main road and secreted themselves in the thick woods. The wounded, however, were still at Sam's disposal. During the whole war they had never been mean enough to imitate their enemies by killing wounded soldiers. In this case the wounded were placed at the house of a widow who promised to take care of them until the Federals at Pilot Knob could have them removed.

Sam's party secured a wagon and loaded it with the booty. They took their own six wounded men and started back to Greene County, Arkansas, where they found all things right at headquarters.

CHAPTER 20

After spending the winter very agreeably, on the 10th day of March, 1864, Sam decided to make a raid in the vicinity of Jackson, Cape Girardeau County, Missouri, with fifteen men, several of whom were from that area and acquainted with the people. This trip was for the purpose of remunerating these men for their services rendered to Sam in the past.

They passed through Butler County into Stoddard, leaving Bloomfield a few miles to the south, then crossed the southeast corner of Bollinger into Cape Girardeau. They traveled slowly and altogether at night, so they created no disturbance and interfered with nobody, making no demonstrations until they were ready to return. In the latter part of the night they arrived in the vicinity of Jackson, selected a good place, and camped for the day. During that time some of the boys visited friends.

One of these men, who was a stranger in that part of the land, went into town to get whiskey and to see what was going on. Upon returning late in the evening he reported that three Federals there seemed to be well acquainted with the people. He wanted to take some of the boys and go back after them, to which Sam consented. They started off in eager haste and soon returned with three prisoners, having met them in the road some distance from town. They were retained as prisoners until the boys who knew them returned. Upon their advice, Sam released two of the Federals and kept the third as a prisoner. He was taken along when the whole company started that night for White Water, but he was not taken far before he was tied to a tree.

On White Water the gang remained inactive for several days, receiving good treatment from their Southern friends. Some of the men were enabled to visit their relatives. The sun was setting one evening when a citizen came and reported that an hour earlier nine Federals had passed along the road, and it was presumed that they would stop for the night at the first house.

As the night darkened Sam's men were in full pursuit of them. However, on nearing the house they rode slowly and tied their horses in a thicket at some distance, then approached the premises cautiously. It was a double-hewed log house with an open hall between and a small cooking apartment forming an ell to the main building but separated from it by a narrow hall also. The men formed a line around the house and Sam crept to the window to peep into the rooms. Only one was lighted, and in it there was no one but an old lady and some little grandchildren grouped around her. Sam crept around and looked into the kitchen window. To his great joy he saw the Federals eating supper.

Sam took an easy position and found their conversation interesting. They were using vulgar and indecent language to the lady who, aimiably, was waiting upon them. There was an old gentleman seated on a box in a corner of the room being thrown insults and threats of a heinous nature. In silent fear the old man bore their bitter curses without returning a word.

Sam retreated from his position, passed around the circle, and collected his men at the entrance to the kitchen into the open hall, this being the only place of egress. He placed a number of his men on each side. Now he stepped into the door and demanded surrender at his men rushed to the door. Each of the Federals pushed back his chair, at which point Sam cried out that he would shoot any man who attempted to rise from the table with his arms. At that moment he admitted his men. The Federals placed their revolvers on the table and retired according to Sam's command to the farthest end of the room and formed in a line.

By this time the disturbance had aroused the old grandmother who came in, the children screaming in fear and clinging to her dress for protection. They halted at the door in dreadful suspense. The oldest girl, who was about eight years of age, sprang into the room exclaiming, "Well, grandma! If here ain't Uncle Bill!" Then, seizing one of Sam's men by the hand she sobbed, "Oh, Uncle Bill! Don't let the soldiers kill pa!"

The old man at this approached the man who had been recognized by the little girl. He offered his hand slowly to "Uncle Bill" while the tears trickled down his weatherbeaten cheek. He said only, "Gad to see you, Bill."

Bill retained it for about a minute, said nothing, but turned and introduced Major Hildebrand to his relative and to the household generally.

Sam stepped forward to receive the salutation of the old gentleman of whom he had heard so much but knew so little. One of the prisoners at that moment muttered, "A hell of a major."

On casting his eyes along the line Sam saw that they were ready to burst into a derisive laughter. At this Sam ordered one of the rooms forming the main building to be lighted. Stationing his men properly he marched the prisoners out of the kitchen through the little hall into the room of the main building. He returned to the kitchen with the man now known as Uncle Bill to have a talk with the old gentleman while his wife prepared a hasty supper for the guerrillas. The old man took Sam's hand and thanked him for his timely visit. He said the Federals had made several trips here but he had previously eluded their search. He explained that their only charge against him was that he had fed bushwhackers. This time they had entered the house before he saw them, and he had no way of escape.

He wound up by saying, "Well, Major Hildebrand, I am agreeably disappointed at your general appearance. I was led to believe, by hearing of your exploits, that you was a rough-looking customer."

Eight men were left to guard the prisoners while the others hungrily started to eat. After that they marched the prisoners to the fence in front of the house, tied their hands securely behind them and placed them on their horses, tying their feet underneath.

Mounting, Sam and his men started south, leading the horses on which the prisoners rode. They reached a part of the country in which they felt safe as day began to approach. They entered a deep ravine about fifteen miles northeast of Bloomfield. It was covered with thick undergrowth and sheltered by timber. Here they hung the prisoners. They submitted to their fate without a murmur. In fact, during the march they had showed not the least sign of being conquered. They confessed that they were McNeal's men and that in joining the army it was for the purpose of killing Rebels.

After disposing of these prisoners Sam and his men secreted their horses in a dense thicket. Ten of them took stations on a road leading from Benton, Scott County, Missouri, to watch for Federals. After waiting all day and not seeing any, they were about to give up and return to their camps, but early in the evening they discovered five Federals riding slowly toward Bloomfield.

Sam's men, divided into two parties, were stationed about one hundred yards apart. The Federals got nearly opposite the second squad, of which Sam was one. Sam stepped suddenly into the road and demanded surrender. They submitted in alarm, and Sam called up his men. The Federals dismounted and surrendered their arms and horses. Sam marched them off the road and a safe distance into the woods.

One of Sam's men had recognized some old acquaintances among these Federals, and now Sam gave him an opportunity to speak concerning their character. It was here reported that among them were his acquaintances of long standing and that four of them were honorable. These four were released immediately, but the fifth one was hung after his case was explained.

When night came Sam's men mounted and, taking their booty, started back to Arkansas.

CHAPTER 21

Because Sam and all his friends belonged to what they called "The Independent Bushwhacking Department of the Confederate States of America," they were entirely dependent upon their own activities for a livelihood. Naturally, it was necessary for them to plant crops. For nearly two months Crowley's Ridge on which they lived and the adjacent country contained an industrious little community of honest farmers.

The axe was heard in every direction. The smoke from burning brush curled up from a thousand fires. At night little boys and girls made bright fires. All day long women worked with hoes and rakes, having to ignore crying babies. At the time of the planting of onions everybody passed with red eyes, and it seemed that the sight of an onion would bring tears to every eye.

Sam put in a good crop of corn and his wife made a good garden with the help of the children. He always wanted to brag that he had the best wife in the world, but all his friends wanted to claim the same about their own wives.

After plowing his crop over once Sam realized he ought to make another trip into Missouri to dispatch some Federals into eternity, but the outdoor work had made everybody so healthy and happy that they had a hard time working up a memory of their grievances well enough to be willing to set out on a killing expedition. However, on the 25th of May Sam chose nine men for another raid into Missouri. Crossing the St. Francis River at the southwest corner of Stoddard County, they went into Scott County and watched for three days and nights to catch some men they had chosen. When they had been unsuccessful in locating those particular enemies, they went in the direction of Dallas, the county seat of Bollinger.

For a while Sam's men wanted to go back home because nothing exciting was happening, but they agreed to remain with Sam for one more day when he asked them. The following morning they were riding in daylight. They had not proceeded more than four or five miles when they discovered seven Federals riding at full speed toward the town of Dallas, which at that time was garrisoned by about a hundred Dutch soldiers. Sam's men dashed after them, and the race was quite exciting. After about six miles of racing the Rebels began to gain on them. Within a mile of the garrison one of the horses fell, the rider knocked senseless. The Rebels disarmed him and made him mount his horse again and then ride along with them for about two miles into the woods.

The Dutchman seemed very much alarmed and talked furiously in broken English. As soon as they arrived in a well timbered hollow they killed him. Within a few hours they stopped at a friend's house, fed their horses, and were well fed themselves. They then made their way to the Flat Woods in St. François County and remained there for about twenty-four hours. Then they went to the extreme northern part of that county and concealed themselves among the Pike Run hills, the most rugged part of the whole state. These hills were covered with a dense thicket of underbrush, a wild and uninhabited section. These hills are not far from the Big River and so they afforded Sam a good place for a temporary headquarters from which they could go searching for enemies.

A well known friend who was willing to help Sam's enterprise feigned business in several parts of the neighborhood. Returning at night he reported that only two culprits were at home: James Walls and John Baker. Early the next morning Sam stationed himself near the house where both of those men resided. He did not have to wait long before Walls stepped out onto the porch. Sam had failed to get a position near enough the house to make it easy for him to kill him. He was waiting for his victims to approach the wood pile which would have meant that he had only about a hundred yards to shoot with Kill-Devil.

About ten o'clock two other men rode up to the house, alighted and went in. It was a half hour later when they came out with both

Walls and Baker who started in an opposite direction from where Sam was hiding. Sam then changed his position to the opposite side of the house, expecting them to return soon, but the sun had dipped behind the western hills by the time Sam gave up and returned to camp. There the friend who had acted as a spy reported that he had seen Baker and Walls going in the direction of De Soto with two other men. One of them had said to the others "Sam Hildebrand is thought to be in this area. At least, strange and rough-looking men have been seen in public places, and it's thought they must be Hildebrand's men."

At this Sam concluded that any further efforts to kill either Walls or Baker would be fruitless, so he ran the risk of watching the town of Big River Mills where his enemies usually congregated before starting out against him. He therefore took up a station on a bluff overlooking the road from the settlement of his old enemies, about a quarter of a mile below the town and fifty yards from the road. At daylight Sam was ready for business. Various people passed along the road at intervals of fifteen minutes or more, but none of them looked like his enemies. He knew he could easily recognize anyone on his list.

But in the evening he did see a lone man riding slowly toward the town, and he recognized Joe McGahan. He had long felt supreme contempt for that man, for he was one of the men who had dipped his hands into the blood of his brothers. As Sam watched him approach he felt an indescribable joy. As he approached the desired point Sam raised his rifle to his face, placed his finger on the trigger and was nearly in the act of pulling when the man turned his face — and Sam discovered the sad and almost fatal mistake. Instead of being McGahan this man was one by the name of Sharp, a Union man living nearby but one who was highly esteemed by all who knew him. Sam had the impulse to hail him and explain with an apology, but fortunately he refrained.

Then he hastened through the woods back to his retreat among the Pike Run hills and found his men waiting impatiently. They started south and, after midnight, reached the pinery southwest from Farmington and slept there until morning. Their horses were so fagged that it seemed best to swap them off before proceeding on their journey.

During the day they stationed themselves near the plank road between Farmington and Pilot Knob to watch for an opportunity to exchange horses. A large company of Federals passed by, but they were too numerous for Sam's purpose. Toward evening they saw three men approaching on fine-looking horses. The names of these three were Burges, Hughes, and Kelley. They lost no time in capturing this party. To prevent them from reporting too soon, Sam's men forced them to travel with them several miles over the rugged hills and deep ravines.

Their captives were very much alarmed.

Old man Burges begged for his life.

Sam replied, "As long as you three are not Federal soldiers it would be barbarous for us to harm you. We merely have to take your horses, but you can have ours in exchange."

They seemed grateful to be released, and Sam's gang kept near the road leading to Pilot Knob until at sunset they came to Abright's store. This man was a good Union Dutchman and he was not in the habit of crediting bushwhackers, so they robbed his store of everything they wanted and then changed their course under cover of the woods. They traveled eastward all night.

Arriving early in the morning in the area where Mr. Bess resided on White Water, they took a position on the top of a high hill. They had a fine view of the surrounding country and especially of the main road along which the Federals were in the habit of passing from Cape Girardeau to Fredericktown.

In the evening when most of them were sleeping the pickets saw a small squad of soldiers about half a mile off making their way westward. On being awakened Sam's men followed him down to the road, which was skirted by a very thick undergrowth. They secreted themselves in two parties about fifty yards apart. Sam gave orders not to fire on the Federals unless they showed fight or attempted to run. When they got near the second squad Sam's men stepped out into the road and demanded they surrender. The appearance of these hidden men was so sudden that they had no time to draw their weapons. Several of them wheeled their horses for a run but, on discovering themselves covered on that side also, they threw up their hands in token of a willingness to surrender. They were then made to dismount and stack their arms against a tree. After that they were marched into the woods and questioned.

Then Sam told them who he was and at this they seemed pleased, remarking that they had often heard of him and had wanted to see him although they had no desire to be his prisoners.

Sam asked, "Have you heard that I'm in the habit of killing all prisoners?"

"Oh, yes," said their leader. "We have heard that you don't regard the life of a personal enemy as of any value, but we've known several men that you have released and they said you were not the blood-thirsty Hildebrand we'd heard of."

The papers they were able to produce showed that they were neither McNeal's or Leeper's men. Rather they belonged to the command of Colonel Beverage of Cape Girardeau. They were then released and sent off on foot.

Sam then led his men toward Bollinger's Mill. In that vicinity about sunrise they met two Federals who instantly wheeled their horses and dashed through the woods. Not all of Sam's men could pursue them because they were burdened with the horses and arms they had recently collected, but Sam and Captain Snap took two men and followed at full speed, catching them in less than a mile. They threw up their hands while they were about two hundred yards ahead. Sam said afterward that he almost shot them for being such cowards, but they were merely taken prisoner, forced to join the other men camping on an adjacent hill. It was then learned that they were new recruits. This was proved by letters from friends that were found in their pockets.

Sam decided, "They haven't been in the army long enough to have committed many depredations." They were taken along because they were needed to help with the captured horses and material. After the whole party had passed Mingo Swamp these latest captured were released. Then Sam and all his men arrived safely in Greene County, Arkansas, well satisfied.

CHAPTER 22

After a few happy days with his family Sam yielded to the persuasion of Captain Bowman to take a trip to St. François County in Missouri for the purpose of capturing a young man by the name of George Hart who, on a scout with some militia, had killed Captain Bowsman's brother for the sake of capturing his fine horse.

This time the company consisted of nine men. They started on the 20th day of June, 1864, and traveled by night. On the 26th they camped for the day at Wolf Creek, about six miles from Farmington. One man clad in citizen's clothes was sent into Farmington to get a bottle of good old "tangle-foot" and to look around. When night came he had not returned, so Captain Bowman arrested a couple of Dutchmen to get information from them concerning the military force in town. He thought that probably his man had been taken in by the soldiers as a spy. The Dutchmen arrested were Henry Vogus and John Zimmer. They insisted there were no forces in town, that they had seen no soldiers for a month.

They said, "If you don't believe us take us with you into town to see for yourselves."

At that juncture the man who had been sent out returned, and he reported that a company of soldiers had been in town for some time, so it was clear that the Dutchmen had been trying to trap them. A short consultation was therefore enough to seal the fate of these two prisoners. They were hung.

Immediately after this the company passed a short distance from Farmington and stopped at the house of Ross Jelkyl, the Provost Marshal. They helped themselves to a few things that they needed. Some of the party wanted to kill him at the same time, but Sam insisted, "He befriended me on one occasion, so we'll not hurt him now."

From there they went to the residence of Charles Hart where they found his son George who was on Sam's list. Some of the men were stationed at the back door and others demanded entrance at the front. The old man opened the door and obediently struck a light. When George Hart was called upon he appeared. He was asked about the horse he had taken the time he murdered young Bowman, and he replied, "I traded him off and he's out of the country now."

"Well, you're going with us now," Bowman said.

"What do you want to do with me?" he asked.

The answer was, "Wait and see."

When he realized that he was to be killed he offered to do something to save his life, but Captain Bowman asked, "Do you think that anything you can offer would pay for the life of my brother whom you murdered in cold blood?"

They traveled for about eight miles, and during that time George Hart made a complete confession.

At daylight they were about a mile from Big River Mills. Not wanting to be encumbered by the prisoner they took some hickory bark and hung him to a dogwood sapling. One of his feet touched the ground, so they placed it in the fork of a bush. That completed the process of hanging.

Now that the main object of the trip had thus been accomplished, their next move was to get supplies of summer clothing for their families. They decided on taking these from an old meddlesome Union German in Jefferson County. His name was Lepp and he kept a store on a small creek called Swashen. They found the old man in his store and succeeded in getting all they wanted at what they called "a very low figure." They even promised him their return in the future.

They well knew that their operations about Farmington would alarm the forces at Pilot Knob, Farmington, Potosi, and Fredericktown, and that the Iron Mountain contingent would be on their trail. Therefore they decided to travel at night and to get out of that region as quickly as possible, but their plans were in some measure thwarted.

On the way to Lepp's store one of the men had complained of

feeling sick. By the time they had ridden ten miles he became too sick to sit on his horse. The whole company retreated to a cave in the Pike Run hills in order to conceal themselves and their horses and captured goods until their sick comrade could travel. Their situation was indeed critical. Fortunately a Southern friend who lived nearby was able and willing to supply them at night with provisions and horse feed. This friend risked his own life in order to show this courtesy. He even procured the services of a physician who checked the disease within a few days.

During all this time the country was literally flooded with Federal soldiers who rode along the road threatening women and children and killing chickens.

Captain Bowman, Sam, and their men had to remain at the Pike Run hills for seven or eight days before their comrade had recovered sufficiently to mount his horse. Of course he was still quite weak, so it was decided that the whole contingent should travel during daylight. They rode slowly through the woods and avoided the soldiers by keeping away from the public roads and by shunning all places where liquor could be obtained.

When they reached the vicinity of the homes of Sam's brothers-in-law on Flat River, they first met old Isaac, a Negro belonging to Mr. Metts. He was carrying a bridle around his shoulders. As the whole party was at this time dressed in Federal uniforms Isaac naturally thought they were Union soldiers. In answer to their inquiries he made a report implicating the Simms family as well as the Shannons and Sweeneys.

He said, "I'd have reported on them sooner, but I was afraid they'd get Sam Hildebrand to put me out of the way."

It is true that the report he had made, if given to a squad of Federals, would have consigned those Southerners to an ignominious death without any further evidence. He had said that in his opinion "if Sam Hildebrand was to call at their houses and ask for something to eat they'd feed him till he was as plump as a stuffed turkey."

Some members of the company, upon hearing this, wanted to shoot old Isaac to keep him from making such a report to the Federals. But Sam said, "The sound of a gun might lead to our discovery."

So they quietly lashed him to a horse they were leading, took him among the hills over toward Westover's mill, and hung him. On searching his pockets for a knife they found a pocketbook containing sixty-four dollars.

Some of the company said, "Since Negroes seem to have money, maybe we'd better catch a few of them until our own pockets are replenished."

The next day they were traveling slowly through one of the woods when they came across another Negro. It was important that they should get through this country without being reported. Having no rope they hung this Negro with hickory bark, but on searching his pockets they found nothing but a cob pipe.

Nothing else of note occurred until they reached the vicinity of Greenville. While camped for the day on a high hill they discovered two men coming up toward them. Because they might have been tracking them it seemed wise to shoot them, but it was soon discovered that they were not armed. They were walking up the hill as though they were tired, and they were within fifteen steps of the camp before they discovered the strangers. Their first impulse was to run, but when they were ordered to surrender they had to give in. It turned out that they were deserters from the Federal army at Ironton, and they were trying to make their way to their homes at New Madrid. One of Sam's men was acquainted with them, and to him they were indebted for their lives. They were detained until night and then permitted to continue on the way to their homes.

It was from them that Sam's men heard some of the horrible tales of pillage and bloodshed that were being reported daily at the Federal camps about Sam Hildebrand. The strangest part of all this was that many of those atrocities were said to have been committed on the same day in remote localities.

Under cover of darkness some of the company proceeded to Arkansas, but Captain Bowman, Traster, and Sam decided to go into Shannon County after a couple of deserters who, in the early part of the war, had belonged to Captain Bowman's command. They had never been of any service, being too cowardly to fight and too lazy to steal, but since their desertion they had constantly been reporting every squad of Rebels that entered that section of the country. They were always willing to annoy the Southern citizens in that neighborhood.

On reaching that place it was learned that they had gone to Ironton, perhaps for the purpose of joining the Union army. However, by the next day they had returned and were quietly captured. Without creating any alarm they were marched back to Greene County, Arkansas, and were hung in the presence of the command.

CHAPTER 23

A man by the name of Gibson arrived in the little Greene County Confederacy for the purpose of joining the "bushwhacking department." He seemed to have some superior advantages over most of Captain Bolin's men because he had a good education and had a way of making men like him. Besides, he was the best marksman among them with the exception of Sam Hildebrand.

On the 16th of July, Sam selected Gibson and eight other men for another trip into St. François County. Although the last few sorties in that direction had not been particularly successful, there was no use failing to try again. It was true that the Union men numbered thousands of armed soldiers in a territory extending 150 miles south of their nest on Big River and were backed by a great nation of untold wealth. Yet Sam felt backed by the South with her armies of 300,000 men. He had no commissary department, no steam presses running night and day striking off greenbacks, no outlets to other nations by commercial treaties, nobody willing to be saddled by a debt of three or four thousand millions of dollars. His long marches had to be made at night and with the utmost caution. The woods were his home, the moon his orbit of light, the hooting owls his spectators.

On this expedition they passed quietly through Butler County, along the western line of Madison, then through St. François and across

Big River to the hills and hunting grounds of Sam's boyhood known as the Pike Run hills. These hills look like the fragments of a broken world piled together in confusion and terminating in an abrupt bluff on the margin of Big River. Here there is a cave halfway up the perpendicular rock later known as The Hildebrand Cave. The mouth of it cannot be seen from either the top or the bottom.

These rugged hills were covered with dense forest and wild grape vines. There were many yawning caverns known to hunters and no doubt to many others never seen by the eye of man. This time they took up their abode in one of those caves during the inclement weather. The ground was too soft for them to venture out on horseback on account of the trail that was sure to be left.

Sam always went around the Big River neighborhood on foot as he searched for his enemies. The only one he saw this time was James Craig. One day he saw this man in the act of leaving home on foot. Therefore Sam made a circuit through the woods and stationed himself in advance with the intention of capturing him. He wanted to take him to his cavern so that his comrades could watch him being hanged. But James Craig did not come along as he was expected to do, so Sam missed his game entirely.

The men were getting tired of inaction, so they started out. On going about fifteen miles they reached a place called the Tunnel, on the Iron Mountain Railroad.

At the store of Christopher Lepp they helped themselves to all the articles they could conveniently carry. Then they took the back track to the crossing of Big River near the ruins of the old Hildebrand homestead. They made their way toward Castor Creek, meaning to kill a Negro belonging to Mr. Kinder. This Negro had become notorious for his meddlesome nature and his propensity for reporting white men. On the night of their arrival they found him. To satisfy themselves in regard to his meanness they passed themselves off as Federals and questioned him about his old master. He freely related the many reasons he had for believing that the old man was not loyal to the Union.

Sam asked, "Are you willing for us to kill the old man?"

He answered, "I'd kill him myself if you would see me out of trouble about it. Some soldiers told me months ago that if I should kill him I could have the farm," but so far he had not found the right opportunity.

At this Sam and his men were sure that the Negro would make good food for the buzzards, so they hung him for that purpose and hurried away.

The only known photo of Sam Hildebrand.

Carl Breihan Collection

They were now travelling in the daytime and going in a leisurely manner. About four o'clock in the evening they were trailed and caught up by a company of Federals. They seemed very anxious for the honor of killing Sam. On getting over the backbone of a ridge they made a rush. When they had gotten to the top of the hill they were within a hundred yards of Sam's group. Their elevation caused them to overshoot all of the men except one poor fellow, a new recruit who was shot in the head. Of course Sam and his men dashed into the brush and covered that rough country at about a mile a minute. They then gave up their horses to the other men with directions where to meet them after the foray. Gibson, Sam, and two others started back on foot to bushwhack the enemy.

Upon getting within 200 yards of the spot where their dead man lay, they saw the Federals exulting over their victory. Sam directed his men to make their way around and take position along the road where they could get a good shot while Sam took it upon himself to run them back. He crawled up to within 100 yards of the party, got a bead on one of them. When Sam fired the man fell off his horse within a few feet of here the other man lay. This put them on their back track, and they went off at full speed. As they passed Sam's men they all fired in turn, Gibson bringing one of them to the ground. But Sam was sure the other boys with him missed their aim although they insisted to the last that they had each wounded a man.

Sam secured the two horses that had belonged to the two men killed and all of them continued their journey. On the following morning they took up quarters within eight miles of Bloomfield.

During the day Sam and Bill Rucker walked down to a plum thicket near the road. While they were there eating plums they saw two Dutchmen dressed in civilian clothes walking by. They called to invite them to have some plums and they readily accepted. As the plum eaters were wearing Federal uniforms of course they were considered Union soldiers. They asked the strangers what command they belonged to, who they were, and why they were not in the service.

They replied that they belonged to Leeper's command and were on furlough and meaning to visit their uncle at Mine LaMotte. They said they were wearing borrowed clothes in order to fool any Rebels they might encounter. They recited quite a good deal about "Bolin's and Hildebrand's band of murderers and ropers," as they called them.

Sam's men shot them both, and in a few days the bushwhackers arrived safely at their usual place for crossing the St. Francis. They arrived on the bank of the river just after dark and were startled to find a camp on the other side at the mouth of a little creek. It was easy to see the reflection of several campfires among the trees, and they caught the sound of human voices. Could it be possible that the Federals were camping there? If so why had they not set out their pickets? Sam could not understand it.

They quietly rode back into the timbered bottom and continued their way down the country at some distance from the river until they were about a mile below that surprising camp, and there they swam across the river. They continued up the river for a short distance, then rode to a high brushy point and dismounted. Then, taking it on foot, Sam proceeded to spy out the mysterious camp above them. He approached it cautiously, watching out for pickets. Finally he stood in the midst of perhaps a dozen little brush shanties without a single human being. More puzzled than ever he peeped into one of the brush arbors and a lady's voice called out, "Who is that?"

The alarm spread, and Sam then heard the voices of women in every direction.

And then to his great surprise he heard the voice of his wife. When she saw him of course she greeted him joyously and was able to explain the calamity which had fallen their community during his absence.

CHAPTER 24

A few days before Sam's arrival in Arkansas the little community of women and children at headquarters was suddenly aroused from their slumbers early one morning by the firing of a gun. They found themselves surrounded by a whole company of Federals under the command of Captain John from Ironton, Missouri.

All the men were absent on various scouting expeditions except for eight who happened to be in camp that morning. They seized their guns and tried to make their escape, but seven of them were shot and only one made his escape unhurt. The Federals immediately commenced burning the houses, after taking all the provisions and clothing they could find.

Of course the women were in great consternation. But they gathered their children and, in their night clothes, huddled together in the center of the square. They were helpless while watching the flames devour their homes. However, before all the houses had been burned Captain John ordered his men to supply the women with whatever clothing they could snatch from the flames.

After their hasty gathering of clothing their terror subsided, and then with perfect composure they watched the progress of the flames without betraying any emotion. They wanted to deprive the Federals of the satisfaction of believing they had triumphed over their spirit of enmity against the Federal cause.

Some of the boys of that community had been out on a hunt, and as they returned the Federals fired upon them, killing two of them. The scouts were in the habit of coming in from various directions, and it was now impossible to warn them before they had arrived in the Federal trap. However, a few hours later the Federals had left, and the women in squads of five or six went in different directions and camped a few miles off to meet the scouts who had not yet returned.

Sam's wife and her party had camped near the St. Francis River and were living on fish when Sam found them to his great surprise. The Federals were still not very far away, burning the farm houses, the mills, and the shops.

As soon as Sam had heard this news he sent all his men out in different directions to ferret out the enemy and to meet with him at a designated place before daylight. With much difficulty they succeeded in finding several squads of the Federals. Naturally, finding the Rebel men absent from where their families were settled, the Federals had divided into many small bands to devastate the country as suddenly as possible.

Sam's scouts met at the time and place designated and realized that their only chance was to bushwhack the Federals to drive them out of this part of the country as quickly as possible. Two men were detailed to take a trip up Black River to notify Captain Bolin and his men so that they might intercept the Federals and bushwhack them after Sam had succeeded in routing them out of that area.

In less than an hour Sam's company numbered fifteen men. They hastened on foot to the lower end of the settlement. When they arrived within half a mile of a farmhouse they found about fifty Federals burning buildings. At the sound of a gun's discharge they turned in that direction and saw a Federal reel in his saddle and fall to the earth. Two soldiers on horseback immediately dashed toward the point from where the shot had proceeded, and they saw a boy about thirteen years old crawl out of a gully and start toward the point of the hill where Sam's men were — with the soldiers running after him.

The boy had such a good start that it was clear he could reach the Rebels before the Federals could overtake him. Sam and his men lay concealed in the thick brush and let the boy pass without seeing them. The soldiers were soon in the midst of the men hiding. They rose and forced them to surrender without creating an alarm. Their captive soldiers were tied securely, and Sam's men then awaited the approach of others who might be sent in search of these two.

The boy was overjoyed when he found out who was there to help.

It was not very long before ten Federals came riding up. The two prisoners had by then been removed back half a mile and quietly hung to avoid their giving an alarm. The arriving Federals met with a sudden charge from rifles, and six of them dropped from their horses. The others wheeled and made their escape.

The other soldiers hastened to an adjoining ridge and kept up a harmless fire against Sam's company for two or three hours, although the distance made their firing useless. No doubt they did this to divert attention, for a fresh force of Federals, numbering perhaps forty men, commenced a deadly fire in Sam's rear, driving him and his men from their position. Naturally their retreat was disorderly. Before they had succeeded in crossing the ravine and gaining the opposite ridge four of Sam's men had been killed and two others wounded. They continued their retreat for five miles. Then they placed themselves to rake the Federals without danger to themselves.

This continued for several hours. They were unwilling to leave, but it became clear that the Federals were planning to burn out the neighborhood, then to attack before the Rebels could collect for a retreat.

They wound their way through the woods to their old headquarters. Late in the evening there was more firing, and they hastened in that direction. They diverged to the right and let the Federals rush past without attracting their attention.

On the following night the Rebels continued to bushwhack the Federals until they had killed eight or ten of their pickets. The next morning the Federals seemed to have taken up their march back to Missouri. During the whole day the Rebels posted themselves in position where they could pick off the Federals as they went by. Late in the evening the Federals made an attempt to follow the Rebels into the woods, but they were attacked on every side, and the slaughter was terrible. Finally they were put to rout after Captain John himself had fallen.

Wearied by the constant fighting Sam and his men returned to their former camp, leaving a fresh group of men with Captain Bolin to continue harrassing the Federals until they should return to Ironton. However, the Rebels had been left in a deplorable condition. They were without shelter for their families except for a few huts that the Federals had not bothered to burn. In each of these two or three families huddled without bedding or change of clothing and with almost no food. Under such conditions some of the children died.

The men had to raid some of the border counties of Missouri in their effort to get supplies for their own families, and many friends provided bedding and provisions. Whenever possible the men branched out far enough to rob the stores of Union men. There was an entire absence of surgical care, the result of which meant that many of the soldiers were forever afterward rendered unfit for active duty.

The whole available force of this Rebel community now amounted to only eighty men. By the time they had rebuilt twenty houses and a temporary mill, the numbers were further reduced by desertions, many of the men leaving to get into Texas for the sake of safety. It was decided that half of the men left should take the field against enemies in Missouri to make them pay for the damage they had caused. In planning this, though, it was never countenanced to apply the torch to dwellings of the Federals, for the Rebels were never making war upon women and children.

Sam started to Washington County in Missouri with fourteen men especially to obtain supplies of clothing and ammunition. They made their way up Black River through Butler and Reynolds counties and entered Washington County on the extreme southern line, traveling only by night and each day concealing themselves among the rugged hills of Black River.

In one neighborhood they had taken several horses, and they then found a store from which they commandeered shoes, domestics, and calicoes. They even found some concealed ammunition which they appropriated. On starting back they traveled slowly. Not having heard of any Federals in the neighborhood they felt safe and planned to travel by day, being familiar with the roads and byways on the way back to Arkansas. But in this they were disappointed. They had gone only a short distance in Reynolds County when they were attacked by twenty or twenty-five Federals who had trailed them from the store they had robbed and now dashed upon them with fury.

Because the Rebels were heavily packed and encumbered with the horses they were leading, they could not run. At their fire one of the Rebels was killed. Sam took advantage of their momentarily empty guns by wheeling his men into the brush and dismounting. In an instant they were able to return the fire, during which three of the Union men fell. Sam dashed forward and about half his men succeeded in gaining the enemy's rear. In a charge against them Sam's men killed two more and wounded several, but two of his own were injured although not mortally.

All the Federals got away with the exception of eight taken prisoner, three of whom were wounded. The dead now counted were five dead Federalists, with a bounty of thirteen horses, eighteen rifles and ten revolvers for the Rebels. Of the Rebels one man was killed and two wounded but not too seriously to delay their traveling. Sam turned his attention to the prisoners who were dismounted, disarmed, and sitting by the roadside under guard.

On his approach two of them rose, called Sam by name, and asked permission to shake hands with him. After a short conversation it turned out that they were two of the men Sam had conquered on Lost Creek in Wayne County during the month of May, 1863. Sam had released them after negotiating with them for the release of Captain Bolin's men who were at that time imprisoned at Ironton. On recognizing them Sam gave them his hand in reassurance that he appreciated the service they had rendered at that previous time. After that little ceremony Sam released those two Union friends together with three of their wounded comrades.

Sam said, "I have to take the other three along with me because I need their assistance in carrying our stock. But for your sakes when we get to Greenville I shall release them."

True to his word that is what he did.

The contingent then hurried to Greene County, being too much burdened to bushwhack any of the citizens who had accompanied Captain John in the earlier rampage. For the present they were allowed to rest. Just the same, having accidentally met one of them on the road, Sam shot him through the head and rode on.

Once back at their headquarters they discovered that things were once again cheerful, and they divided their goods among the needy families.

CHAPTER 25

In the latter part of August, 1864, Sam selected four men and started after some of his old enemies on Big River. By this time they had all disappeared except three or four who spent their time around the Federal camps. Sam had not lost sight of those of the old mob who must have thought they were dwelling in safety. He kept himself posted in regard to their movements. The special object of this particular trip was to penetrate the enemy country as far as De Soto in Jefferson County, Missouri, to surprise a couple of the old mob who now lived in that vicinity. He hoped that before the authorities should become aware of his unexpected presence he might succeed in his little mission of vengeance.

On passing Bloomfield it was true that they were within the Federal lines. A heavy military force had been stationed at Pilot Knob at the beginning of the war, and later smaller forces were stationed at the county seats throughout Southeast Missouri. They were inactive as far as the national war was concerned, but they amused themselves by marauding and occasionally killing unarmed citizens.

On arriving near Fredericktown Sam and his men obtained important information from friends there relative to the distribution of Federal forces. This helped them to shape their course. They went east to Mine La Motte and took up quarters for the day in an unfrequented place about three miles south of the Cross Roads in St. François County. They remained unmolested until evening, when they discovered a man in Federal uniform slowly tracking their horses across an adjoining bridge. When he came within a hundred yards of Sam and commenced making his way toward the camp Sam turned Kill-Devil upon him. Owing to his stooping posture in looking for tracks he was shot too low and broken down in the back. He set up a hideous yelling so Sam had to dispatch him with his revolver.

It was then to be expected that some attention might have been attracted and that perhaps a Union force might be on the track, so Sam and his men had to move. Directing their way through the most thickly wooded areas they reached Wolf Creek about midnight at the plank road leading from Farmington to Ste. Genevieve.

By this time Sam's men were much fatigued from lack of sleep, so they decided to camp until the following night. Fortunately they had with them sufficient provisions and horse feed. They slept soundly until daylight, then did picket duty by turns until late in the evening, when two Federal soldiers were discovered in the valley below evidently on their way to Farmington. They were surprised when Sam and another of his men demanded their surrender. After dismounting and disarming them they were removed to a quiet nook in the woods and interrogated. They reported that they belonged to a company at Ste. Genevieve under Captain Milks. This company had formerly been stationed at Farmington, harrassing and robbing peaceable citizens in that community.

Sam knew that on one of their scoutings through the country the soldiers had arrested Charles Burks, county judge of Ste. Genevieve, for compelling the Provost Marshal to return some horses belonging to the judge. After his arrest by Milks' men, Judge Charles Burks was shot without questioning and without even a charge of disloyalty having been made against him.

On another occasion Milks' men had arrested Irvin M. Haile, one of the most peaceable men in St. François County, under a charge made by some sneaking informer, that on one occasion he had fed one of Sam's men. He was allowed no trial, no defense, but was led off a few miles and shot through the head. His body was left where it lay and his horse was taken.

The recollection of several such atrocities committed by that particular company gave Sam no choice but to kill these two men and throw their bodies into a deep hole in Wolf Creek with stones tied to their feet.

As soon as it was dark Sam and his men went to the house of a friend to get some food. On arrival they saw a party of about twenty soldiers mounting their horses in front of the friend's gate and riding off into the darkness. Sam approached the house cautiously and found nobody there except a kind lady who explained that "Sam Hildebrand is supposed to be in the neighborhood." Some soldiers from Fredericktown had come to search for him and had ordered citizens to ride out and assist them.

After getting something to eat and feed for their horses Sam's contingent started off. By daylight the following morning they were safe in a cave among the Pike Run hills in the northern part of St. François County. There they remained but a day and, as soon as darkness approached, they traveled into Jefferson County until about ten o'clock. Then they stopped at a house where a friend gave them supper. He warned them against going any farther in the direction of De Soto, but they did not take his advice very seriously. Unfortunately, while making a forced march between daylight and sunrise on an old unfrequented road near the top of a ridge where they were planning to take up quarters until dark, they ran into a company of Federals.

They charged on sight, firing a volley, but Sam's group miraculously escaped unhurt. Their furious charge had caused Sam's men to scatter. After a hasty retreat of half a mile or more Sam stopped and looked around at his surroundings. He hardly knew where he was after that exciting fifteen minutes, and neither did he know what had happened to his men. But it was clear that there were no Federal soldiers in sight.

Sam had designated a place in the Pike Run hills for his men to meet in any emergency of this kind. He struck out for that spot, keeping within the most thickly timbered country.

Arriving late in the evening Sam found that one of his men had arrived a short time before. Together they waited in suspense and had almost come to the conclusion that the other men had been captured or killed when they came up. They had gotten together soon after the stampede and had become lost. But at dark they had pressed a river pilot into their service as he was passing them along the road. The pilot Sam knew very well. He carefully deceived the pilot about the course he and his men were now about to take and then released him when he promised not to report them.

However, it was now clear that they would be hunted down like wild beasts in a forest, so they resolved to get out of the country as rapidly as possible. They knew they had to cover some country that they had not used earlier. They started in a westward direction and after traveling a few miles stopped at the house of a friend for supper. Then, crossing the Iron Mountain railroad south of Blackwell's Station, they gained the vicinity of Old Mines in Washington County before it was yet light. There they took up quarters for the day. Because one of their number was acquainted with that neighborhood they had no trouble in collecting necessary provisions and horse feed.

While making that brief sojourn an amusing incident occurred. About ten o'clock in the forenoon, while it was Sam's turn to stand on picket, he sauntered through the brush down to the main road distant about 200 yards. Suddenly he ran on to a German who was sitting near the roadside, sheltered from the sun by some brush. He held in his hand an old double-barreled shotgun and was wearing a worn Federal uniform. He had not seen Sam approaching, and of course Sam immediately drew his revolver. The German sprang to his feet, let his old gun fall to the ground and threw up his hands.

Seeing that Sam too was wearing a Federal uniform he tried in a hurried broken English to give an account of himself. He said he was from De Soto and was on the way to a sawmill west of Potosi, that he was a discharged Union soldier, that Sam Hildebrand was in the country near De Soto and that he was afraid to stay there on that account.

At this Sam extended his hand, saying, "I was a little bit frightened because I thought you were Sam Hildebrand. I shall not hurt you if you are a Union man. But I came very near shooting you under the mistaken idea that you were Sam Hildebrand."

At this he laughed heartily and showed himself quite merry indeed.

Sam then said, "Some of Sam Hildebrand's men are stationed back in the woods. Why don't you come with me and form one of my party for the day?"

He gladly consented and gratefully followed Sam through the thick brush.

Sam said, "You're running a great risk in traveling in this part of the country, for it is one of Hildebrand's main passways."

As they reached the boys in camp he did not wait for an introduction but stepped in ahead of Sam and shook hands with them all, gleefully telling them that he was acquainted with Sam Hildebrand. The boys seemed to catch on immediately, and then humored the German, even asking him absurd questions about Sam's barbarism. The old man answered the questions assuring them that Sam was really a bloodthirsty barbarian without an equal in the world's history.

It was not until later in the afternoon that they gave their identities. It was hard for the German to comprehend the sudden change and realize that he was in the hands of the feared barbarian. At last, however, he became convinced and began to give out a series of lies that would have shamed Baron Munchhausen. Finally Sam's men stopped him short and assured him that, if he would not report them, they would let him go. Then, seizing Sam's hand with both of his, he pledged himself and swore by all that was holy that he never would report the gang while he lived. He then shook hands with all of them. He looked back every ten feet to be sure he was not being followed. Then he doubled his speed until he was out of their hearing.

While the sun was yet an hour high they started on their way, keeping to the woods until dark, then passing west of Potosi. By traveling all night they reached a point near the town of Centreville in Reynolds County. There they obtained food for themselves and their horses.

In traveling down Black River late one evening they ran into a squad of six Federals, whom they charged furiously, firing upon them with revolvers. They did not return the fire but ran most ingloriously. One was killed and two others captured. Those captured stated that they belonged to Leeper's command, so of course they were shot.

Confiscating their horses and arms before another night's journey, Sam and his men arrived safely in Greene County, Arkansas. There awaiting for Sam was a dispatch from General Sterling Price requesting him to take charge of the advance guard of his army since he was "going up to possess Missouri." Sam gladly consented on condition that the General would release him as soon as they should reach the vicinity of his old home on Big River.

CHAPTER 26

During General Price's raid into Missouri in September of 1864, by request Sam took charge of the advance guard after all arrangements had been made for the grand campaign. He felt that a great honor had thus been conferred upon him, and he hoped to be enabled to triumph over his enemies and to establish himself at the home of his childhood. With these daydreams he arrived at the appointed place and found that his command consisted of a party of ragged Missourians, about forty in number, some of whom he knew personally.

Keeping pace with the main body of the army, they traveled not more than fifteen miles a day. Nothing of importance occurred until they reached the town of Doniphan in Ripley County, Missouri. On approaching that place, large volumes of smoke were arising from the town. Putting spurs to the horses they hastened into the place and found the Federals evacuating, having set fire to every house but one, and that belonged to a Federal officer. Sam concluded that that house also deserved to burn. He had arrived, however, in time to save the mill. McNeal's and Leeper's men were by that time on their way to burn up the whole Greene County Confederacy. However, hearing that General Price was on his march in this direction they set fire to the town and decamped.

Sam's group pursued and overtook them before they reached

Greenville. In the skirmish two men were killed and four wounded. They captured sixteen Federals and shot them, rushed on to the town of Patterson, captured eleven Negroes and seven white men in Federal uniforms and shot them. While the main army under Price was advancing, Sam scouted in front of them with his command. Union men in that area were now scarce, as Sam held the advance, passing through Greenville, Bloomfield, Fredericktown, and Farmington. All of these places were evacuated before his arrival, and he passed through them with his force without molesting anyone — with one exception. On reaching Farmington he found that no resistance was offered. Although the people were alarmed they all surrendered quietly — except for a German named Abright. He ran as Sam approached, refused to halt when commanded to do so, and was shot as he ran.

Finally, upon reaching the Iron Mountain Railroad at Mineral Point, Sam's men burned several bridges and tore down the telegraph. Finding no resistance and according to a previous understanding with General Price, Sam hastened to the neighborhood of his personal enemies. Finding they had all fled, Sam employed himself in recruiting for the Southern army. In the short space of six days he succeeded in getting a full company. They were sworn into the Southern service under Captain Holmes.

During this particular chore Sam was at the residence of Major Dick Berryman, the stone house in Bogey's Lead Mines near Big River, with a portion of Captain Holmes' men, when four Federals who had escaped from the fort at Ironton during the siege came along the road. With but little difficulty Sam's men effected their capture, shot them, and threw their bodies into a mineral hole.

The main army did not remain long in that section of the country. General Price was a great military chieftain, but his campaign through Missouri seemed to lack design. From the time he entered the state until he left it he garrisoned no posts in the rear. Pilot Knob, the terminus of the railroad from St. Louis and the depot for supplies for all Southeast Missouri, was taken and then abandoned the next day. He made his way to the Missouri River and then up that stream in the direction of Kansas for several hundred miles without molestation, leaving St. Louis, the great commercial key of the West, almost "spoiling to be taken." He left St. Louis to his right, while the heavy force at that place quietly took possession of the abandoned posts in his rear. If he had joined the "Independent Bushwhacking Department of the Confederate States of America" with all his men, in less than thirty days there would not have been a Federal soldier west of the Mississippi. While Major Berryman and a few other officers stayed in St. François

County recruiting, the main army gained the Missouri River and quietly made a blind march in the direction of Idaho.

The Federal forces took possession of the Iron Mountain Railroad, and on one pleasant afternoon in October the new recruits, armed with their shotguns and squirrel rifles, were run into by Major Montgomery of the Sixth Missouri Cavalry and completely routed, in which event their loss was seven killed and all the balance missing. Montgomery also killed several citizens whose names were Fite, Vandover, and Judge Haile, the father of Irvine M. Haile who had previously been murdered by Milks' men.

On the day before Major Montgomery routed the new recruits at Big River Mills, Sam went with some men to Cadet on the railroad and took from the store of Mr. Kellerman a wagon load of goods which he delivered up to Major Berryman. He, in his turn, distributed these goods among his men. Major Montgomery, with two companies of the Sixth Missouri Cavalry, struck their trail and followed them nearly into camp. But when he ran into the pickets they obeyed the orders Sam had given and ran in a different direction from the camp, thereby leading the Federals away from the squad of raw recruits and giving them time to escape.

Sam was not at Big River Mills when Montgomery stormed the place, but he was at St. Joseph Lead Mines when he passed. Sam was sitting on his horse talking to a lady when he saw Montgomery's men within a few yards. He assumed an air of unconcern and continued the conversation. Upon noticing that he was being eyed, Sam turned his horse and rode within a few feet of the column. Then he turned his horse and rode within a few feet of the column in the direction they were going, talking back to the lady until he was too far off to continue the conversation. He then found himself near a lieutenant whom he addressed as captain, asking in an awkward manner if he was going to Big River Mills to drive the Rebels off. He answered in the affirmative.

Sam then said, "I should like to help you if only I had a gun."

The lieutenant replied, "I want no men who are not drilled."

Sam's horse then gave the appearance of being a little lame, so he gradually fell back, talking all the time to the man opposite until the last one had passed. He then "cussed" his horse in an apparent effort to keep up with the column but showed impatience because he could not keep up. Upon being left about a hundred yards behind he suddenly took the opportunity to slip into the woods. The lameness of his horse was amazingly much improved, but he could not beat the column into town. However, he knew that the pickets would obey his instructions and lead them off some other way. They did so but were overtaken and killed at the ford above the mill pond.

The new recruits were within hearing of the guns and "broke for tall timber." The short sojourn of the Confederate forces in Missouri was indeed a severe blow to the course Sam had marked out for himself. In his imagination he had raised the veil and looked down the vista of time to behold the Southern arms triumphant, the country again restored to peace and prosperity, his little family and his aged mother leaning upon his arm for support at the old homestead, surrounded by all the endearments of the once happy days of slavery. But he was awakened from that dream upon the termination of General Price's raid.

His mind was impressed with the fact that the people of Missouri were tired of war and would sacrifice but little more to the shrine of their political convictions. In fact a large majority of them were compelled by circumstances beyond their control to remain at home and take their chances. The atrocities committed in their midst by men professing Union sentiments finally failed to elicit from them even a casual remark.

At the beginning of the war the American people had been untutored in regard to the cruelties of war. In fact, no nation on earth had the remotest conception of the cruelties of American fighters, Northern and Southern, with all their boasted moral and religious training. It turned out that political words expressed in time of peace many years before the war commenced were later used against citizens, and their lives forfeited as a result.

Through his native woods Sam traveled alone to his home in Arkansas, his fond hopes crushed, his spirits below zero.

CHAPTER 27

Sam could not accept defeat until he actually had to. After recruiting the horses and making necessary arrangements for the comfort of his family in his absence, he selected three men and set out for Madison County, Missouri, expressly for the purpose of killing the German who had reported on the preacher Polk and by whose instigation Polk's murder by the Union soldiers had been brought about.

The venerable Baptist minister, William Polk, was about seventy years of age and had been preaching for about forty years. No man ever stood higher as a Christian. As a citizen his conduct was irreproachable. As to his loyalty and patriotism it could never have been brought into question. Actually, from his lips no word had ever dropped that could have been construed as an expression of the Southern rebellion. Still, in the latter part of October, 1864, three Federal soldiers rode up to his house first to rob him and then to kill him. When he gave them the money they demanded (it amounted to twenty dollars) they replied that this amount was not enough to save his life.

They took him out of the house, and a Federal soldier named Robert Manning shot him through the head. Sam had reason to believe that the German informer was the most guilty person in that transaction, and he was willing to attempt the German's capture even at this inclement season of the year. Camping in the woods was disagreeable. Stopping at the homes of friends at night was dangerous. And if a snow should happen to fall the trail would be exposed to the Federals, in which case it might be necessary to run a horse race for nearly 200 miles.

On reaching the St. Francis they found it swollen from recent rains. Sam swam it and arrived safely at the opposite bank. But his three men had entered the river too close together, crowding their horses. That caused them to beat down the current until one of the men, the one named Swan, washed into a drift and was nearly drowned before Sam could remove his coat and boots and swim to the scene. Sam did reach him in time to drag him out of the drift, but his horse was washed under and never seen again.

After crossing they built a fire, dried their clothes, and camped for the night. The next morning Swan did not feel well, so he decided to make his way back to headquarters, while the rest of them proceeded as planned. They traveled only twenty or twenty-five miles a day, stopping with friends on the way.

On reaching Madison County they were on the lookout for Federal squads, knowing that two or three hundred troops were quartered in Fredericktown. Inasmuch as Sam's ammunition was getting scarce, it seemed he would have to stop to see some friend in town. They secreted themselves and their horses about a mile from the place and, as daylight was near, they had to lay over for a day. On the ensuing night Sam made his way cautiously and crawled into an alley near the residence of his friend, when a dog tried to make him retreat. At first he tried to negotiate with the dog, but all to no purpose. At about ten o'clock he went around the opposite side of town and started in through an open street, walking leisurely but keeping close to the buildings.

When he had gotten fairly into town he came upon a Federal picket, who inquired, "Where you going, Bill?"

Sam answered in a whisper, "After some whiskey."

"All right," the picket answered. "Bring me a snort."

Sam soon came to a large saloon and passed around to the other side which was closed. He spent several minutes by looking through the window. He saw quite a few Federals, some playing cards, others amusing themselves in various ways, all enjoying themselves. He made his way to the friend he was seeking, climbed over the plank fence, and gave the secret wrap at the back door. He got the lunch and some good brandy, plenty of ammunition, and rations to last two days, as well as some valuable information. He then returned to his comrades by the smaller alleys where usually only the small dogs were likely to be met.

By this time the night was half spent, so Sam and his comrades went into the neighborhood of Mr. O'Banyon and camped in the woods until the following evening. At that time they made their way over to the accused German.

Dressed in the Federal uniforms they rode up to the German's house as the sun was setting. They were received cordially, and they talked to him for a short time when the subject of Preacher Polk came up. In a boastful manner the German gave the history of his transaction in the matter, fully confirming his complicity. He was then marched off into the woods near the farm of Mr. North. Sam made him understand that "hog killing time" had come and shot him.

As soon as it was dark enough they rode back to the suburbs of Fredericktown for the purpose of silencing a certain Union citizen there who had made himself officious in reporting citizens for disloyalty and for accusing certain others of having "fed Sam Hildebrand." Sam left one of his men with the horses and took the other to knock at the door he was looking for. Their knock was answered by a lady who innocently told them that the man they were asking for had gone to St. Louis. They bade her good night and left the town.

They hurried on to Castor Creek and stayed with a friend for several days while they were trying to locate another man. But evidently the excitement raised by the death of the German was making this intended victim shy. When they did go to his house after dark one night his wife assured them he was not at home. Despite searching every room they did not find him.

They then started for Cape Girardeau County in order to obtain some supplies for the winter. They succeeded in getting all they could conveniently pack, and then started back to Arkansas.

They encountered one squad of Federals on the homeward trip, just as they were passing through Stoddard County, east of Bloomfield. A party of ten soldiers came up behind them and fired upon them before they got near enough to do any harm. By taking to the woods they made their escape. If they had been pursued they might have been forced to throw away their goods, but fortunately they never were in danger again. Nevertheless, their horses were quite jaded by the time dark came and they were having to go slowly. They swam the St. Francis without much trouble and landed safely at home.

He found his wife and children well, but Swan, whom Sam had rescued from the turbulent waters, had reached home quite sickened and had died.

CHAPTER 28

Sam had a long conversation about the probable termination of the war with Captain Bolin, who had just returned from an expedition on the headwaters of Current River. He was a man of considerable intelligence, and Sam had noticed that always on his return from a raid his pockets were stuffed with Yankee newspapers. This morning he was sitting on a log deeply absorbed in his kind of reading.

"Well, Captain," said Sam. "What's the news from the North? Are they ready to give it up yet?"

"Give it up, indeed, Sam! The war is very near to a close."

"I thought so," said Sam. "I knew they could not hold out much longer. I suppose we have killed nearly half of them. I hope they will grin and bear it until we get another swipe at them."

"Sam, it is the South that is going under. Her fate is already sealed."

"What makes you think so?"

"The great armies of the Confederacy are crippled and almost annihilated. Their whole country is overrun and impoverished by by immense Northern armies. I fear that our great chieftains will be compelled to yield, and when they go under our little fighting here must also stop."

"Ah, Captain! You get that from those Yankee papers. I can't believe anything they say."

However, Sam was staggered by Captain Bolin's remarks. He immediately selected four men, determined to make another trip to see if the Federals had really swallowed up the whole country. They made their way up Black River hoping to go a long way without ever meeting a Federal.

One evening, on the first day of March, 1865, after remaining in a thicket all day, they approached the house of a friend with whom they had previously stopped. A rainstorm was coming up, and they wanted to leave their horses where they were while they themselves repaired to safe shelter. Their friend was not at home, having gone toward Springfield looking for his son who, he feared, may have been murdered by one of the roving bands of Federals. A good woman told them that none of the enemy had passed that way for a long time. Feeling perfectly safe they went to the barn, hoping to get a little sleep. But they took the precaution to crawl up into the loft and over the hay into a low place near the wall.

Directly after dark they were awakened by the noise of a large empty wagon being driven up to the barn just under their window. On peeping out they discovered that not less than fifty Federal soldiers were in the barn yard all around them. On watching their maneuvers a few minutes they became satisfied that they knew nothing of their presence.

The barn floor below them was soon full of them. Within a few minutes eight or ten of them had crawled up through the window on the hay and rolled up in their blankets between Sam's men and the window. Their escape seemed impossible. They might lie still and escape detection for a while, but as soon as it was light the Feds would load their wagon with the hay and be sure to discover the strangers hidden there. Sam was at his wit's end.

In this predicament he and his men lay quietly for two hours, when all at once they heard the fire alarm, the good woman in the house lustily calling for help. In the corner of the yard about fifty feet from the house there stood a little cabin that had once been her dwelling but was at this time used for stacking boxes and barrels. That little building was in flames. Afterwards Sam learned that she herself had set it on fire to draw the soldiers from the barn so that he and his men might effect their escape. In this she succeeded admirably. The soldiers broke for the fire to prevent it from catching the main building, while Sam and his men made their escape.

Once free and back where they had left their horses they took a deep breath, mounted, and managed a good night's travel. They passed near the town of Buford, then went west to Fredericktown. When they

The Union's Brigadier-General Thomas Ewing, Jr., who issued Order No. 11 after Quantrill's raid on Lawrence, Kansas.

Kansas State Historical Society

arrived in the vicinity of Flat Woods they remained concealed in a thick forest all day. In the evening, two of the men dressed in the Federal uniform wandered off from camp. They were discovered by a citizen named John Myers who of course took them for Union soldiers and commenced telling them how he had deceived the Rebels.

As a matter of fact this John Myers handed Sam's men a sheet of paper on which he had written a full report of his success in ferreting out the friends of Sam Hildebrand in that neighborhood. He declared that he was in the habit of reporting to the Rebels also and, to prove this, he drew from his pocket a half-worn paper purporting to be an account of the Federal movements in that section of the country. He showed a strong desire for the capture of Sam Hildebrand. Sam's men then told him that Sam Hildebrand had already been captured and was a prisoner at their camp nearby. Thereupon he waved his hat and shouted like an Indian.

To satisfy his curiosity they took him into their camp. Immediately noticing that Sam was not tied he tried to make a retreat, but he was stopped. As soon as night approached he was shot.

Then Sam and his men proceeded toward Big River. They stopped in the pinery northwest from Farmington and remained there for two days. On leaving that point they took supper with a friend near Big River Mills before going down the river to the old Hildebrand homestead. Some friends had built old Mrs. Hildebrand a cabin on the premises which she had long owned, and it was suiting her purpose as a temporary abode, and here Sam found her on the night of March 6th, 1865.

He left men and horses in a secure place nearby and quietly approached the place where he had spent his boyhood. It was late in the night, but his mother had not retired. On hearing her son's voice she laid her spectacles on the Bible she had been reading and softly opened the door. Her motherly arms that had so often clasped him to her bosom even now made him feel secure from the storms of life. He could not help contrasting her condition of the old days with her poverty of this cheerless present. There was however a calm serenity in her face. A quiet resignation seemed to pervade her nature. Considering the terrible loss she had sustained — death of her sons and the uprooting of all her cherished hopes — Sam was about to express his wonder. She understood his thoughts and made a slight motion of her hand toward the Bible.

In a faltering tone she said, "My dear boy, you are more unhappy than I am."

Sam remained with her during most of the following day. She

told him that it was her impression that the war was near its close, that the Union triumph was about complete. She told him that when the Rebels should lay down their arms it would be wise for him too to yield obedience to the government and claim its protection. Sam was so softened that he almost forgot his enemies. He agreed to return to Arkansas without killing anyone if he could do so without sacrificing his own safety.

But it was necessary that he and his men should collect some goods for their families who at this time were greatly in need. They made a raid into the town of Big River Mills, starting late in the evening, keeping along the main road, and arriving in town between sundown and dark. At the store of J. V. Tyler they helped themselves to such articles as they needed and then hurried on all that night, getting as far beyond the travel road as possible.

The next day they rested, but at two o'clock in the morning they discovered a force of Federals was on their trail as they wound around a hill. They could plainly see the movements of the Federals as they followed Sam's tactics of making a circuit, and he made his escape by the same method. Very cautiously they started down the hill in the opposite direction, rode about three miles, made another circuit, and went on in a great hurry. Every few miles they made a similar curve before continuing. By the time they had made their last circuit they were far beyond the enemy's reach.

They had no more trouble with the Federals and reached Arkansas with all their goods which were needed by their families.

CHAPTER 29

About the first of April, 1865, Sam started toward Missouri with four men, one of whom was Tom Haile. They passed west of Bloomfield attempting to take in a German, living on the edge of Wayne County, whose name Sam never could pronounce. He had rendered himself obnoxious by carrying news to the Federal authorities.

On going up to his house at sunrise, thinking he was asleep, they made no concealment of themselves but marched directly to the front door. When they had gotten to within a hundred and fifty yards he ran out and struck across a little field. Sam's men shot their guns at him, one at a time, and he squalled like a panther. This ticked Tom so well that he could not shoot. He laughed aloud as the German yelled. They cared so little about him that they made no attempt to pursue him.

They marched toward Fredericktown, reaching there about daybreak, and secreted themselves during the day while Haile went alone into Fredericktown.

He walked into town swinging from his shoulder a stick upon which hung an old coat and a dirty cotton handkerchief. He passed himself off as a lame Irishman who wanted a job for a few days. He met several acquaintances who very kindly passed him without showing any sign of recognition. However, it later appeared that while they had been passing Mr. Blake's farm someone had recognized them and had reported to the soldiers. A company was ordered out to guard a gap where the Rebels had been known to pass.

Sam had distinctly heard horses' feet on the gravel road where he and his men lay concealed the thick forest awaiting the approach of night. Immediately after dark they started off and, on crossing the gravel road, they were fired upon from a short distance. They dashed through the thick brush but Sam's horse got tangled in a grapevine and his men left him while he was vainly attempting to get the horse through.

The firing became rapid, and Sam was making too much noise trying to get through the tangled brush. He dismounted, knowing that he was completely surrounded but also that the enemy lines were yet at some distance. He dropped the bridle over a snag and ran back about a hundred yards. He stepped behind a bush and remained very still, knowing that if he should fire they would see the flash of his pistol.

They were closing up in regular order toward the point where Sam's horse stood. They were soon within a few steps of Sam's hiding place, facing toward the horse which gave a snort. Sam took a few steps and then called out in a commanding tone, "Advance with more caution. They can hear you a mile."

By this time Sam was in their line. He stepped behind them and got away without creating their suspicion. Upon being discovered by the guard holding their horses, he said, "We've got the bushwhackers surrounded. To make a sure thing of them we need more men."

Mounting the best horse there, Sam, in the dim light of the moon, started toward Fredericktown in a great hurry. When out of danger he changed his course for Simms' Mountain in St. François County, the place designated as the meeting place for his men in case of trouble. No doubt the Federals captured Sam's entangled horse, but he had obtained a much better one.

He rode all night and part of the following day before he reached the place of rendezvous. His men had not arrived, and as the day wore on he began to fear they had met with some misfortune. But they did make their appearance after dark, and they reported that the Federals had given them a severe chase. Besides, they had met another squad of Federals who had followed them when they rode in the opposite direction. That explained their delay in reaching this point of rendezvous.

Simms' Mountain is a high level of land scarcely ever visited by any but hunters and then only at certain seasons. It affords a splendid view of the surrounding country. While the men lay there Tom Haile took a trip to Iron Mountain to learn the news of the military camp as well as to get provisions. After leaving his horse and arms at a certain place he stopped at an old coal pit to smut his face and hands. Then, disguised as a collier, of whom there were many in the neighborhood, he went into town. While purchasing supplies at a store he learned that 500 soldiers had Sam Hildebrand surrounded in a thicket from which it was impossible for him to escape.

This was good news, for it would enable Sam and his men to make a raid on Big River in broad daylight with perfect impunity. They passed Flat River during the latter part of the night, crossed Big River at the Haile Ford, and rode into town just as the sun was rising. Finding no goods there that suited them, they continued along the main road until they reached the residence of their good Union friend, Robert Hill. They wanted to pay him a friendly visit, but Tom Haile insisted that they should not do him any personal injury.

Sam took two of his best horses and left two in their place. They also took some clothing and other articles that could be useful. They then turned south and passed along the most public road four or five miles until they came to Nesbit Orson's. There they took a fancy to a couple of mares that some neighbors had left there, one belonging to Tom Highley and the other to Tom Crunkelton, as they well knew. However, the mare which they took evidently did not like Rebels, for on getting along a few miles she had thrown all Sam's men, one at a time. When Sam himself was about to try his luck the mare broke away and made her escape.

Tom Haile had remained behind in order to visit some of his friends on Big River, and he did not overtake the party until they had reached the Cook settlement. Sam and the others continued to travel along the road until they reached the shanty belonging to an old Negro by the name of Jim. He had made himself the dread of Southern sympathizers by frequently visiting the different military posts with various charges against his neighbors such as feeding bushwhackers. To satisfy himself as to this man's complicity Sam and his men rode up to his cabin, all dressed in the Federal uniform. They called him out and gave him a hearty handshake and inquired if he had learned anything more about a man named Madkins that he had been talking about at the Knob. At this he imagined he was recognizing Sam as a certain colonel, and he asked, "What have you done to your shoulderstraps?"

Sam replied, "Oh, I need to find out a few things for myself, so don't tell anybody about my disguised appearance."

Jim then made charges against several of the Confederate men in the neighborhood to consign them to Federal punishment. Then he asked, "Are you still willing to take my son as a waiting boy?"

Sam replied, "Sure, and I was planning to take him along right now if that's all right with you. In fact, I've brought along a horse for that purpose."

He called the boy out and told him to mount the horse. At first the boy refused, but after Sam had gotten the father to mount another horse for the purpose of going along a few miles, the boy consented and seemed reconciled. After they had ridden two miles they shot old Jim but took the boy on with them.

They stopped near the residence of Francis Clark in Cook settlement to get their dinners. While they were there some Federals came along, but on seeing Sam and his men in their Federal uniforms went around without stopping. They then proceeded without meeting with trouble and after that traveled only in the night.

On reaching the St. Francis River they found it still out of its banks. They managed to swim it by resting the horses on an island about halfway across. From there they arrived safely at home — and for the first time in his life Sam "owned" another human being. That made him a genuine southern slaveholder.

Robert Hill became satisfied that, considering that Sam had taken his horses, he could no longer pass himself off as both a Rebel and a Union man. He was a member of the "union League." He went before the provost marshal at Potosi and declared that in consequence of his Union sentiments he could not live at home on Big River without a band of soldiers for his protection.

Failing, however, in this purpose, he went to Ironton and made a similar statement to the provost marshal at that place. Certain Union men knew the facts in his case and represented the matter as arising from personal enmity against Dr. A. W. Keith and others.

Thwarted again in his designs, Robert Hill, after musing over his misfortunes for a few days, had the bright idea that he would expose the "Knights of the Golden Circle" and consign his brother members to butchery.

The war was nearly at an end. The Union cause was about to triumph, and one string was enough to play on during the balance of the struggle. Hill sought and obtained a private interview with the provost marshal. Spring had come and men throughout the world were plodding on in their daily pursuits. Robert Hill told the provost marshal that he was a member of the Union League. This announcement proved his loyalty, for this Northern League had been instituted to protect the National Union secretly. He then announced that, for the good of his country, he had also joined the Knights of the Golden Circle which met at the house of Joseph Herrod on Big River, that many of the leading men in the neighborhood were members.

His statements to the provost marshal had the effect of a telegram sent to Colonel Beverage at Cape Girardeau, who sent Lieutenant Brown with forty men to Big River Mills. They discovered no conspiracy, however, and Robert Hill's revelation had no serious effect.

CHAPTER 30

When the war had first broken out in Missouri and after the persecutions against the Hildebrand family had become intolerable, Sam had been unable to pay a smal debt he owed to D. W. Taylor, a merchant living at Valley's Mines in Jefferson County. Taylor had attached Sam's interest in the Hildebrand homestead and had sold it at public venue, himself bidding it in for a nominal sum. For this little piece of ingenuity Sam now determined to award him a clear title to another tract of land, four by six feet.

With this intention, about the 28th of April, 1865, Sam started with four men for another raid on Missouri, all of which was now held by Federal authorities. Reaching Big River late in the night they repaired to the Pike Run hills and slept until morning, when they rode about six miles over to Taylor's store. He was not at home and, having no time to lose, they went into his store to select whatever they wanted.

Suddenly they were run onto by some Federal soldiers under Lieutenant Brown from Perry County, who was now stationed at Big River Mills with forty men, half of whom he had with him on this occasion.

They came within 200 yards of the store and commenced firing and yelling. Sam and his men ran out to their horses which were tied to the brush not more than forty yards off but on the opposite side from the soldiers. One of Sam's men was killed and another (a new recruit) left his horse and ran off into the woods, leaving Sam with an "army" of only two men to repel the attack. The Federals, after their first attack, took refuge behind some old houses about 150 yards off. From there they showed a harmless and cowardly fight. After Sam got to his own horse he used him for fortification and shot several rounds at them. Occasionally he could see one head bob around a corner but they were out of range and Sam's shots fell harmlessly to the ground. His other two men now left him alone, and for several minutes he continued to try to get a dead shot at one of the Federals. Having no chance to do so, he mounted his horse and retreated, leaving his dead man on the ground. He then went to an adjoining hill, but failing to find his men he rattled his cowbell and within half an hour his three men had joined him.

After this failure they felt chagrined and started south with the Federals trailing them. Once again they went to the Pike Run hills for safety. From there they could easily have whipped all the forces within three surrounding counties.

Sam's comrade went on foot four miles away to the house of an old acquaintance and borrowed a horse, promising to return him in six weeks (which promise he faithfully kept). It was now the middle of May, and they were anxious to be on their way back home. They started one night and went as far as Flat Woods.

There Sam had earlier become acquainted with George Miller and Joseph Johnson, whom he believed to be his good friends. For some reason never learned, they later (after Sam's expulsion from that neighborhood) went to his wife's house and used vile language. Johnson told her that he intended to kill Sam and would bring his head to her swinging from the horn of his saddle. This was not a vain threat, for after that they watched for Sam but he never saw either of them after he learned of their threat.

Late one evening, as Sam was passing a certain house, he saw a lady making some butter. Wishing for a drink of buttermilk he alighted and went to the house. He was wearing a Federal uniform so the lady asked if he was out searching for Sam Hildebrand.

He replied, "Yes."

She then went on to give him details of the affray at Taylor's store, ascribing to the Federals a brilliant victory against the outlaws.

She said, "Lieutenant Brown, with only twenty men, ran upon Hildebrand's bushwhackers and completely routed them, killing fourteen and wounding several more. A great many soldiers are out for Hildebrand now, and they have surrounded him in a place where he can never get back to bother us again."

Sam asked, "Would you please give Sam Hildebrand a drink of buttermilk?"

She stared for a moment and then replied, "Yes, sir. You can have all in the churn if you want it."

Not long after leaving there Sam found Mr. Miller in his field and shot him. After dark he found Mr. Johnson at home, took him out of the house, and cut off his head with a bowie knife. But he did not attempt to carry his head to his wife swinging to the horn of his saddle. Instead of doing that Sam pursued his way home to Greene County, Arkansas.

On the day after his arrival at home Captain Bolin called on him and said that he wanted all the men to meet him at headquarters that evening. At the time appointed Sam was there and so were about forty others of the boys, most of whom had just returned from their various scouts. The Captain seemed agitated, and for several minutes after they were assembled he did not say a word.

Then he said, "Gentlemen, it is my wish that we remain quietly at headquarters for a few days until my other scouting parties return. I wish to say to you now that, in my opinion, the war has virtually closed. General Lee, the great head and front of all our hopes, as you are aware, has succumbed to superior numbers and surrendered on the 9th day of April. General Johnston surrendered on the 18th of the same month. The hopes held out by General Kirby Smith in his general order issued at Shreveport can never be realized.

"The Southern Confederacy is at an end. Our course must be governed by circumstances over which we have no control.

"The course we have pursued during the struggle is justified only by the fact that a great war existed. While the eyes of the world have been riveted upon great actors and on events of an astounding magnitude, the minor details of the struggle have been overlooked. That condition of affairs no longer exists. The war has ceased, and our operations must cease too.

"Finally, it is my request that each and every one of you submit manfully to the same terms that have been forced upon our great chieftains: that is, lay down your arms, surrender on parole, and return to the pursuits of peace."

This little speech fell like a wet blanket on these men, and on Sam most of all. He and all the men held Captain Bolin in such high esteem that not a murmur of dissent dropped from the lips of any man there. However, on the next day there was full discussion in every camp. Nine-tenths of the men fully endorsed Captain Bolin's statements but

Sam was annoyed that the war had ceased before he had finished fighting. He knew little and cared less about the political problem that the war had been expected to solve, nor whether the States formed the Union or the Union formed the States; whether the South had inherent rights or whether inherent rights had the South; whether the General Government was a restricted agent of the people or whether the people were the agents of the General Government.

The practical question with Sam was, "Are all the scoundrels killed off or not?"

Most of the men who had composed the Vigilante Committee on Big River were still alive. Sam's mind was troubled by the reflection that they would now crawl out of their hiding places, swing their hats, and cry out, "Well, didn't we whip them!"

Sam made up his mind that he would take as many of the boys as wanted to refuse surrender and escape to Texas. They could fight under General Kirby Smith and then make their way to Mexico, from there annoying the Federal Government all they could.

However, he knew that he had to consult his wife to see what she thought of such a plan. As a matter of fact, when Margaret heard his idea she looked serious for a minute, and then she burst into laughter.

She said, "I once heard of some little boys who were left home by their parents who went to church. One of the little boys discovered a rat that had taken refuge under a pile of lumber in the yard. The boys tore away the lumber, splitting some of the boards. The rat then ran under the ash-hopper, and when that was torn down the rat took refuge under the barn floor. One of the boys ran to the house for matches in order to burn out the rat. But his little sister, the youngest among the children, said, 'If you burn out the rat you will burn the barn down, and then we'll have no barn.' The boys saw the force of her reasoning and they let the rat go. I advise you to make no further efforts toward destroying the Federal barn."

When his wife made this little speech Sam felt that it contained more good sense than he had heard in a long time. Suddenly he was determined to follow her advice. She had waded through the hardships of war with a strong devotion to her husband. He knew he ought to respect her comfort. On the following day he told Captain Bolin that he consented to the orders given.

Captain Bolin then started on to Jacksonport to turn in a list of his men. A few days later Sam followed him and received his parole on the 26th day of May, 1865, the very day on which General Kirby Smith surrendered at Shreveport.

The war now being over, Sam tried to banish the subject from his mind. Soon he went to work on the place he still occupied, for no owner had appeared to claim it. Most of his men were afraid to return to their homes in Missouri while a remembrance of their depredations and brutality were fresh in the minds of the people, so they went to farming in different parts of Greene County. Of course Sam had far less than half as much as he had owned before the Vigilante mob had worked against him. Sam had resorted to plunder to sustain himself while he pursued the object of killing his enemies. He and his pals had sustained themselves during the whole war at the expense of their enemies.

"If objections are made to that kind of warfare," said Sam, "I can point to the example of Sherman in Georgia and to a host of other Federal commanders, even down to the Big River Militia. Of course we did not charge our government. Never was I a burden to the Confederacy to the amount of one dollar."

So at the close of the war, and in fact during its continuance, Sam and his family were in strained circumstances. He went to work and raised a good crop of corn and everything else they needed. In the spring of 1866 he rented another place in a better locality and farmed on a larger scale. At the close of 1867 he was rendering himself and family as comfortable as could have been expected. The Negro boy he had taken from Free Jim in St. François County still remained with Sam, free but with no family other than the Hildebrands.

CHAPTER 31

Early in the spring of 1868 Sam put in a good crop of corn and devoted much of his time to gardening. His prospects looked good indeed, better than those of many others, and the Negro man still worked for him cheerfully.

Early in the month of April, 1868, one of his old war associates, with whom he had passed many a hardship, came to see Sam and stated that he had received bad news from his home. His sister had been deserted without cause, and the fellow had taken up with a Negro woman, living with her not ten miles away. He asked Sam to help him take the couple out for a good flogging. Something had been said about the fact that such a couple ought to be tied together. Two or three days later that guilty pair were taken from a mill pond, drowned but still tied together. Sam's friend's wife told about the conversation, and suspicion rested upon him and Sam.

Major Sarge came with three men and arrested Sam and his friend, taking them before the authorities. After the preliminary hearing they were both lodged in the jail at Jacksonport. They were secured by handcuffs and by ball and chain. Their escape was therefore impossible. Some Negroes came by the prison and said they ought to be hung by a mob. They were so strongly guarded that Sam doubted the possibility that any of his friends could ever release them.

In June Sam's brother William, who had served during the war with the Union army, came down to Arkansas for the purpose of taking Sam's family back to Big River in Missouri, for it looked as though his wife would soon be a widow. She sold the crop as it stood on the ground for what she could get, and she hired a teamster to haul the family to Big River. In fact, she made the trip in safety, arriving at the old homestead with Sam's mother and brother William.

Sam's prison life every day became more intolerable. He was in jail for four months and had almost abandoned hopes of ever being released. On the last day of August, as he lay brooding in a helpless condition, at about dark someone whispered through the grating: "Be of good cheer. Tomorrow night we are coming to release you if we possibly can."

By rare good fortune, the next night when Sam's friends lay in wait, a boat landed at the wharf. It attracted the attention of all the populace, and Sam with his friend were freed from jail without any disturbance. Sam was so overjoyed at being free that he leaped off the platform in the dark and sprained his ankle. He was in a bad fix for traveling, but soon they were out of danger. He rode until daylight, then they all scattered, each one taking his own course.

Sam hobbled on his way, living on nothing but May-apples until he had covered about thirty-five miles. There at the house of an old friend he remained until he was in good condition. Then he started to go to where his family was, in Missouri. He found them at his mother's home on Big River and remained for a few weeks. But it became clear that his presence in that neighborhood was anything but pleasant to his old enemies, so he removed to Illinois and settled on the Mississippi about forty miles below St. Louis. There he went chopping cordwood for a living, fully determined to withhold his hand from the commission of any act that would indicate anything but that he was a law-abiding citizen.

In January, 1869, he moved across the river on the Missouri side, at a place called Rush Tower. He continued cutting wood until the first of April, when he rented a small farm owned by Samuel B. Herrod on Three Rivers in Ste. Genevieve County near the county line of St. François, about four miles from Big River Mills. To this place he removed his family. His oldest son was twelve years old, and on him fell most of the labor of the farm.

Sam's arrival seemed to create a panic among his former enemies. No doubt they continued to fear retribution. Though Sam had no such intentions, the neighbors secretly went to work to effect his destruction.

Sam was informed that Joe McGahan took several trips to

influence the Governor of Missouri to crush him out of existence. Governor McClurg instructed Colonel Myers, Police Commissioner of St. Louis, to send out men for Sam's arrest. In May, 1869, the commissioner sent McQueen and Colonel Bowen, who were met at Irondale by Joe McGahan, to direct them to Sam's place. However, after they had traveled about ten miles daylight overtook them.

McGahan said, "To be seen here in daylight will be dangerous for me," so he left the others, went home, and never returned.

At the approach of night the detectives were obliged to proceed without a guide, on foot and in a strange neighborhood. They wandered around all night and waded Big River at a deep ford. Then they were obliged to pass another day in the woods. As they could not find Sam's whereabouts without further information, one of them, disguised as a rude country man in search of employment, managed to get the information he wanted. They watched around Sam's house for eight days and nights. Their provisions gave out. Not being able to get any food from Sam's former enemies, they started back to Irondale at ten o'clock one night. From there they took the cars to St. Louis.

While this was going on Sam was working at the mouth of Isle Bois on the Mississippi.

It was known in some circles that during the war Governor Fletcher had offered a reward of $300 for Sam's capture. This and other rewards were offered at the time, and about now some people wrote to Governor McClurg to ask whether the reward was still valid. On being advised in the affirmative, James McLaine, for one, prowled around Sam's house for a whole month for the purpose of trying to win that reward.

On the night of June 6, 1869, Sam ventured up to his house at a late hour to see his family, and remained with them all night. In the morning when he stepped out into the yard he heard the report of a gun from a cluster of hazel brush about eighty yards off. In returning to the house for his gun he discovered that he had been shot through the fleshy part of his thigh.

By the time he returned to the garden the person who had fired had run away, so Sam went to Mr. Pratt's stable a short distance off. McLaine passed by with his gun. After going up to Sam's house he came back and passed along the road not far from where Sam was standing in the stable. Believing that he was the assassin, Sam almost shot him but was prevented from doing so by Mr. Pratt.

Sam was then taken to the house of William M. Highley who went after a physician to have Sam's wound dressed. It proved to be a serious wound and disabled Sam for a long time in such a manner that he was not able to walk. After that he was hauled to Samuel Gossam's house and then to the residence of his uncle, John Williams.

This uncle's family consisted of himself, Aunt Mary, and a granddaughter about six years of age. His house was among the hills in the western part of St. François County, five miles from Big River Mills and one mile due south from the stone house formerly occupied by Dick Berryman. Sam's uncle lived in a log house one story high, consisting of one room. In the yard to the west stood a dilapidated cabin with torn-down chimney, near which stood the smoke-house and a cluster of cherry trees. Opposite the south end of the house, at a distance of aobut eighty yards, was the spring house.

Sam's crippled condition lasted a long time and caused him great anguish. For many months he believed that he had been shot by James McLaine, but later learned it was by Cyrus A. Peterson from Fredericktown and that he had been accompanied by Walter E. Evans. He had never harmed either of those men. He did not even know Peterson, and Evans he had met casually a few weeks earlier and had shaken hands with him.

The Evans family resided on Big River only a few miles from the Hildebrand homestead. The Evans widow and her daughter remained safely at home during the entire war. Although most of the family was known to be Unionist, two of the sons, Ellis G. and William C. Evans, were uncompromising Unionists. Dick Berryman had once told his men that he would not suffer them to interfere with the widow Evans or her property. According to this command Sam had governed himself.

There was a rumor that Sam had died of his wounds while he lay in bed at his uncle's. One night Sheriff Breckinridge and a party of about six men, thinking they might yet collect the bounty without any personal danger, got near to Mr. Highley's house and crept behind a gate-post. They called out Mr. Highley, who assured them that Sam was not on the premises. Just the same, they made a charge on the house while Mrs. Highley was donning her dress. Breckinridge thrust his gun against her dress and thrust it to the other side of the room as if it might have been hiding their quarry.

From there they went searching for Sam — and found him about daylight at his Uncle Williams' home. His uncle was at the crib, so they made him march ahead of them toward the house with their guns loaded, of course. Sam saw all this and fastened the front door, refusing to open it upon their demand. Sam fired four shots at them before they had fired at all. One tumbled behind the ash-hopper and the others dashed around the house. Their shots struck the wall at the back of the house a few inches over the bed where the little granddaughter lay. She gave a horrible yell, and Aunt Mary ran to her.

"Come away with me," Sam said. "Both of you stand in that corner. Bring her a piece of pie to stop her from crying so that I can hear what's going on."

Sam managed to get two more shots through the crack near the chimney, one toward Noah Williams as he stood in the chimney corner hunting for a crack. But Sam found the crack first and sent a shot across his breast, tearing his clothes in such a manner that he left in disgust. The others kept firing through the door. The beds were literally riddled, and Aunt Mary got one bullet on her chin. Next a whole volley was fired through the door, and she was scraped on the head with five holes through her dress.

Then they marched the old man in front of them to the door, and he stood with his right hand against the door, crying out, "Sam, open the door or they will kill me."

"Hold on, Uncle," Sam replied. "Step out of the way."

Just then Sam opened the door with his arms crossed, firing right and left with his pistols. He shot Breckinridge in the groin and another man through the shoulder. Andy Bean broke into a run and jumped the fence just as a shot passed through his red whiskers grazing his face enough to saturate them so that he looked like a stream of blood. The whole party now leaped the fence while firing, and one shot went through the uncle's wrist.

The man wounded in the shoulder was taken to the spring to have water poured on his wound. Breckinridge was taken to Frank Simms to have his wound treated. Andy Bean was taken to Ironton to have the arteries around his beard dressed. Sam's Aunt Mary then brought Sam a bucket of water and left the house, saying, "There are enough provisions in the house to last a week."

Telegraphic dispatches were then sent to St. Louis, to Potosi, and to Farmington for more men. James McLaine and Dennis O'Leary came from Farmington, and Captain Todd Hunter arrived with eight or ten men from Potosi and Irondale. From a hill 200 yards off they kept up occasional fire at the house during the balance of the day. The party behind the spring house had to remain there on account of Sam's shots. However, they kept up a random fire to show that they were not yet dead. Once they held a hat around the corner of the house as a test, and the hat immediately got a hole in it.

While the firing continued Sam tried to cook some dinner for himself. He ate heartily, then rested a while before going on duty again. About sunset McLaine climbed upon the old cabin and after kindling a fire on the roof he climbed down and stood near the door on the far side of the cabin. By a lucky chance Sam shot him dead. This created great excitement, and as his men crowded around his body, Sam crawled out of the back door among the weeds and through the fence. He was not able to carry his gun because of his wounded leg, so he had to leave it. He crawled through the woods for about two miles, for by this time darkness was favoring his escape. Arriving at the house of a friend he obtained a horse and rode to the home of his sister, Mrs. Adams, who lived near the old Hildebrand homestead.

Sam had to stay in a cool place on account of his wound, so he went to a cave he knew in the Big River bluff, half a mile north of the residence of G. W. Murphy, near the Pike Run hills. There he remained for some time, provisions being brought to him every day by his sister. During that time his wife and children were watched so closely that they were unable to visit him.

CHAPTER 32

There were constant police operations carried on for Sam's capture or destruction. A few days after the fight at Williams', a detective with a dirty face and hair uncombed, riding an old mule with a pack saddle and blind bridle, went to Big River Mills and inquired of Dr. Keith and Samuel B. Herrod where Sam Hildebrand was, explaining that he was an old chum of Sam's who wanted to help him. His ragged coat and old hat must have identified him at once as a detective, and he failed to elicit any information. During all this time Sam was nursing his wounds, visited only by his sister.

The Police Comissioner of St. Louis sent Colonel Bowen and McQueen, Schuster, and Wadkins on a second expedition against Sam. At Irondale they were joined by Hughes, King, Patchet, and Zoleman and at Big River Joe McGahan and Dennis O'Leary joined them. On the 21st of June, just before daylight, Colonel Bowen with his men went to the house of Sam's sister to question her. She refused to give them any information. They then threatened to hang two of her young sons, and one of them told all he knew, which was not much. On the evening of June 22nd Sam's brother-in-law was arrested along with Mr. Cash and Mr. Dunham and the three of them were hung up by the neck until they gave out the suggestion that Sam was probably living in a cave somewhere. They were finally able to say they didn't know where the cave was but it was probably three hundred feet above the waters of Big River. They may have known that a line of high timber on the margin of the river hid the front of the towering mass from view.

Actually the cave could be seen neither from the top nor bottom, for it was about 200 feet from the bottom and was hidden by a projecting rock. In one direction along the seam of the rock there was a narrow causeway running several hundred yards where it could be approached from above or below. This narrow path could be easily defended by one man against 500. But Sam was not there when Colonel Bowen and his posse were prowling along in front of the cave on the morning of the 23rd. He had retired from that cave the night before they came. On the following night they built a large fire on the projection in front of the cavern and kept it supplied with wood which they threw from the top of the bluff. On the following morning they learned from Mr. Nash, whom they hung by the neck for a while, that Sam was not in the cave.

On receiving this information the party scaled the bluff and took the place by storm.

The next move they made to capture Sam was through a confession made by a son of Mr. Nash that he was going to meet Sam at a certain point at night with a quart of whiskey. So Colonel Bowen and his party reconnoitered for several hours, but Sam kept 200 yards away from them. He did take a hearty drink of the whiskey but left the rest of the bottle for them.

After all that reconnoitering Colonel Bowen made his headquarters at G. W. Murphy's. There he and his boys lived well, drawing good wages and incurring no danger. Sam had promised his friends that he would not kill anyone of them unless they should indeed discover him. Three or four days after Colonel Bowen had captured the bluff, Sam was aiming to cross the road about 300 yards east of Murphy's house when, on getting into a small glade fifteen steps from the road, he heard horses' clatter coming from the direction of Big River Mills. He stood behind a cedar bush with a cocked pistol in each hand. Colonel Bowen rode by with two of his men, but none of them turned his way as they passed.

A few days later Sam hobbled over to where his family was, but on passing through a wheatfield he was discovered by a man who reported him. Colonel Bowen and a squad of his men watched around the house that night. Before arriving there in the dark rain Sam had heard the tramp of horses and had stepped into hiding until they should pass, and he saw them placing their pickets near the house.

After their campaign against Sam had continued for several

weeks, it must have become apparent that the forces already in the field were insufficient for Sam's capture and that the disloyalty of the people of St. François County had been greatly magnified. Certain men desired nothing so much as martial law.

Although Governor McClurg was a good man, he was slow in detecting the designs of some of his party friends who lived in the undercurrent of conspiracy. Sheriff Murphy was ordered, just as the farmers whetted their scythes in preparation for entering their harvest fields, to call out the militia throughout the county to aid in scouring the woods in search of Sam Hildebrand. Then the report circulated that Sam was concealed in a deep mineral shaft among the Pike Run Hills. Sheriff Murphy and his party scrambled over that rough country until they had crushed every snake under their feet.

This severe ordeal was continued for two or three weeks. Then the Governor arrived on Big River and was pleasantly received. Sam wanted to see him because he had never yet seen a governor of any kind. Having been informed that Governor McClurg would be making a speech in Farmington, he posted himself in a fence corner at the end of a lane on the Green place five miles from Farmington. Sam knew the Governor would be coming along this road so he was there to watch for him, never meaning to molest him. He was hoping that the Governor might be alone so that he could step out, shake him by the hand, give him a drink out of his bottle, and have a social chat.

But when he passed Sam he was riding by the side of a Methodist preacher from Caledonia named Williams. He was followed by a train of about forty men, those that Sam thought of as the saints being in front and the sinners in the rear. Sam did not join the procession but rather retired farther back in the woods.

McClurg did make a speech that evening, saying things that were anything but flattering to Sam. He encouraged the citizens who made protestations of holy horror at the mention of the name of Sam Hildebrand. First they agreed that such a man ought to be arrested, then that it would be proper to arrest him, then that to arrest him would be a good idea, and sixteen other suggestions of the same kind. These resolutions were read to Sam a few days later, so he knew that the Governor had appointed six deputy sheriffs for St. François County. Their number was later increased to ten, each of whom was supplied with a posse of ten men. At this Colonel Bowen made a point of having fought the terrible battle single-handedly when he was speaking at the Brick Church on Big River.

Colonel Bowen at one time was passing the Brick Church when he was made aware of some disturbance in the bushes. He later reported that the irrepressible Sam Hildebrand and his band of outlaws had shot his horse from under him but that he had driven the enemy from the field receiving only a slight wound. After that the Colonel returned to St. Louis.

Previous to this, however, by the Colonel's orders, Sam's wife and children had been removed first to Irondale and then to Farmington, and kept at the latter place for a month under the supervision of the sheriff. On a certain night one of Sam's friends named Crittenden went to Farmington with a light wagon. Before the light of day Sam's wife and children were in Ste. Genevieve County on their way to Illinois. They stopped for breakfast at a house by the roadside, and that proved to be the house of the late James McLaine. McLaine's widow, not knowing the party, made them welcome and in excusing the meager fare observed, "I am now left a destitute widow, and all these poor little children are left orphans by the hand of Sam Hildebrand."

Mrs. McLaine's father, George Shumate, was present, and he addressed himself to Crittenden and the woman and children with him, telling of terrible deeds by Sam Hildebrand. After the breakfast the widow refused to accept any recompense for her kindness in entertaining these travelers.

Sam's wife, taking Mrs. McLaine by the hand, said, "Mrs. McLaine, I am truly sorry for you and your dear children, knowing as I do the hardships you have suffered. I know how to sympathize for I myself am a widow."

"You a widow?" "Yes, Mrs. McLaine. I am worse than a widow. I am the wife of Sam Hildebrand."

The good woman stood amazed and said nothing but her father drew up his neck, threw his head back, and stuttered: "Well, my God! But you are not Sam Hildebrand — are you?" staring at Crittenden in fear.

Crittenden said, "No, sir, but his wife here is my cousin."

They continued safely to Illinois, and as soon as all police operations against Sam in Missouri had subsided, he too left the state. From then on he wandered about trying to appear as a peaceable citizen. The Governor's reward for the capture of him was not repealed. Sam once said that it should have been chiseled in the marble pillars of the State capitol as a reward in the same category as rewards to be offered for a feasible northwest passage and for the invention of perpetual motion. He even thought that there might always be a strange flickering light in the dreary lowlands of the South while some "Jack with his lantern" went on forever trying to get a reward for catching Sam Hildebrand.

CHAPTER 33

The quiet little town of Pinckneyville, Illinois, never accustomed to much excitement, was thrown into the throes of wild rumors on the night of March 21, 1872. News reached the residents of that tiny hamlet that the notorious Sam Hildebrand, member of the Missouri guerrilla fighters during the Civil War, had been slain.

Sam and his family had moved into a small room in a house south of the old mill on Tuesday, the 19th of March. He told the owner of the room that he wanted to remain there a week or so, or until he could rent a small farm in the vicinity.

Little attention was paid to this stranger as he strolled around the town on Tuesday, Wednesday, and Thursday, notwithstanding reports that he was the notorious Hildebrand. These rumors were not believed by the townspeople because, wherever Sam went, he was introduced under the name of John Smith.

From existing records it appears that his stranger did reveal his identity to R. Q. Thompson and that he truly was looking for a little farm that he could rent for himself and family. He also had intimated that there were certain parties who, if they knew of his whereabouts, would be glad to liquidate him. He also confided to Thompson that he no longer feared being encountered for the purpose of obtaining the reward earlier offered for his arrest because the time for which that award had been offered had expired.

On Thursday a band of rough-looking men gathered about this character in earnest conversation. Most of them were strangers in town and did not excite any suspicion until the evening when the fracas began which terminated in the death of "John Smith."

About five o'clock of that evening he, in company with several others, entered Joseph Bishop's saloon. One of the group named Sullivan stepped up to the bar and called for liquor to be served the crowd.

At this the proprietor, Bishop, remarked, "You don't have money enough to pay for that number of drinks."

Sullivan shouted, "That's a damned lie!"

At that the stranger said to be Sam Hildebrand rushed forward to the bar, a twelve-inch Bowie knife in his hand. He swung the knife at Bishop, leaving a cut on that man's chin. Then Sam also drew a revolver with his left hand and seemed about to shoot Bishop, when Bishop's wife interfered. She grabbed Sam's hand and, with the assistance of others, succeeded in evicting him from the saloon. Sam put up his pistol and was about to sauntner away when Bill Gordon, the town constable, decided to take him into custody.

At that time the crowd of rough men who had been seen with Sam during the day gathered around him intent on intimidating the lawman to prevent Sam's arrest.

One of the men said, "The man who cut Bishop just ran into that alley."

Constable Gordon replied, "I'm too old a hand at this game to fall for that," as he took hold of Sam's arm.

This attitude of the officer unnerved most of the men gathering around Sam, and no further resistance was offered. Sam, however, shook loose the officer's grasp from his elbow and reached for his revolver. At the same time Constable Gordon struck him with his nightstick, inflicting a gash over Sam's right eye. This blow seemed to subdue Sam who was then taken before the Justice of the Peace Hamilton and charged with violation of a town ordinance. Jim Sullivan, one of Sam's confederates at the moment, was also tried on the same charge. E. H. Lemen and Thomas Boyd were retained as counsel for the defense.

The evidence did not sustain the charge against Sullivan, so his case was dismissed. But "John Smith" was fined. He paid most of the fine right away and was about to leave when the constable insisted on taking him before Justice J. B. Davis, where a warrant had been issued at the request of the State. It was at this point when the desperate struggle commenced — a struggle which ended in the death of Sam Hildebrand, alias John Smith.

Upon reaching the corner opposite the old Sherman House, notwithstanding that officers Rule, Ragland, and Gordon had hold of him, "John Smith" displayed a knife and was about to use it when the weapon was knocked from his grasp. Upon reaching the corner opposite Sullivan's Hotel, the captive displayed a second knife, but then he was knocked down and disarmed.

The officers resumed half-dragging, half-carrying the kicking man toward Justice Davis' office. When they arrived opposite the Masonic Hall he had a third knife in his hand. He struck at Ragland, cutting his trousers in the area of the abdomen. He then struck Ragland in the left thigh, inflicting a gash from the knee to the hip, laying the whole thigh open.

At that point Officer Ragland drew his revolver and shot the prisoner in the head. The bullet went in just behind the left ear and ranged from the neck up into the base of the brain. The grip of the dying man loosened. He staggered a few feet and fell dead. Ragland was attended at his home by three doctors, Beyton, G. P. Johnson, and H. Johnson, and he eventually recovered.

J. B. Davis called an inquest in the matter of the death of "John Smith" who was now disclosed to be Sam Hildebrand.

STATE OF ILLINOIS) SS
PERRY COUNTY)

Be it remembered that I, J. B. Davis, Justice of the Peace in and for said County, on the 21st day of March, A.D. 1872, at the count aforesaid, in pursuance of the statute, in such case made and provided, did, in the absence of the Coroner of said County, summon a jury, and proceeded to hold inquest on the body of one Sam Hildebrand, alias John Smith, whose body was then and there found dead, and the said jury, after having been duly sworn, according to law, and having inquired into all the facts concerning the death of said body, return to me the following verdict, to wit:

STATE OF ILLINOIS) SS
PERRY COUNTY)

We, the jury empaneled and sworn to inquire into the cause of the death of a man whose name is supposed to be John Smith, said to be late of Farmington, Missouri, find from the evidence, that said deceased came to his death by a pistol shot fired by John L. Ragland, in self-defense and while in the discharge of his official duties as Constable of said County.

Witness our hand this 21st day of March, A.D. 1872.

M. C. EDMONDS, Foreman

No one doubted that the dead man had been the notorious Sam Hildebrand. After his death his children freely confessed that fact, giving the names of the grandparents and the place of their father's former residence in Missouri.

Surviving Sam were his six children, the oldest being Henry, age 15. The others were Rebecca, aged 13; Mary Elizabeth, aged 12; Nancy, aged 10; Margaret, aged 6; and George Washington, aged 4. Rebecca gave the name of her grandparents on her mother's side as Henry Hampton and Mary Elizabeth Hampton, saying that their home had been at Flat River, Missouri. The grandparents on her father's side, she said, were George and Rebecca Hildebrand.

The children were polite and did not admit to the name of Hildebrand until the Saturday following their father's death. They stated that their father had used the name of Charlie Thompson from time to time, and that when coming to Illinois he had assumed the name of Smith and had told his children to do likewise.

Why Hildebrand had gone to Illinois was open to question. One source stated that he had gone there to dispose of two men who had been instrumental in capturing some outlaws and counterfeiters. It was hardly realized that he was looking for a place where his family could live peaceably among people not cognizant of his long bloody record. It was noted that Sam's mare, which his son said nobody except Sam could ride or catch, was saddled and waiting in the alley Thursday afternoon. Perhaps Sam had been ready to make a quick getaway if it ever seemed wise to do so.

As in the matter of such outlaws as Jesse James, Billy the Kid, and others, the story of Sam Hildebrand's death at the hands of a constable in Pinckneyville, Illinois, was discredited in many quarters. However, the identification of Sam Hildebrand, known locally as John Smith, was soon established beyond a doubt.

On the third day after his death his body was taken up and photographed by an artist residing in Pinckneyville. A copy of the picture was sent to the Sheriff of Washington County, Missouri, inasmuch as that officer had taken an active part in efforts to arrest Sam two years earlier. That sheriff now declared the portrait to be that

Sam's grave at Elvins, Missouri.

of Sam Hildebrand. The photograph was also shown to persons who had known Sam well. He was identified by William Hildebrand, his brother, who was very much affected and exclaimed, "That's Sam! Anyone who ever knew Sam would know this is his photo. I want a copy for the family."

The picture was also identified by Jacob Ringer, one of his schoolmates, although how he was called this when Sam had gone to school only one day in his life is unknown. A citizen of Irondale, J. W. S. Boyce, also identified the likeness, as did two of his former neighbors, M. Adams and Frank Simms.

Sam was also identified by a conspicuous scar which he had received during a former attempt by officers to arrest him.

On Thursday, March 28th, another Coroner's inquest was called in the matter of Sam's death. Held in the County Courthouse, it confirmed the results previously mentioned.

For many days wreaths of evergreen and flowers were strewn upon the grave — not by his wife or his children or by any family members, but by unknown admirers — perhaps by people whose lives or loved ones he had saved, perhaps by those grateful for his services to the Confederacy. In his short thirty-six years he had been most unusual indeed. If he had not been caught in the coils of war, his phenomenal courage and keen mind could have accomplished great things for his country.

Sam's remains were later removed to the Hampton Cemetery at Elvins, Missouri.

ADDENDUM

The Official Records of the War of the Rebellion, Union and Confederate Armies — 1861-1865, reveal some interesting correspondence which was carried on between various Union officers in Missouri, relative to Sam Hildebrand and his band of bushwhackers.

Report of Col. W. R. Penick, Fifth Missouri State Militia Cavalry
Hdqrs. Fifth Missouri State Militia Cavalry

Independence, Mo., Feb. 11, 1863.

General: On the 8th instant I sent a detachment of 50 men from Companies C, D, and F, of my command, in charge of Lieut. D. A. Colvin, of Company C, in pursuit of a guerrilla camp, of which I had information. My scout came up with the enemy about 2 p.m., and a running fight commenced, which lasted about thirty minutes. My men killed 8 of the guerrillas, wounded 2, and the remainder, some 4 or 5 men, escaped in the woods. Captured all their arms and horses, and lost 1 man in the skirmish. To try the fighting qualities of the Negro, I sent a contraband along, at his own request. My officers and men agree that his fighting propensities are splendid; he was wounded severely in the right shoulder; he expresses his willingness to again fight the bushwhackers as soon as he is able.

Very respectfully
W. R. Penick
Colonel Fifth Missouri State Militia Cavalry
Maj. Gen. Samuel R. Curtis
Commanding Department of the Missouri

Office Provost-Marshal General

St. Louis, Mo., March 19, 1863.

Col. W. Hoffman, Commissary-General of Prisoners.

Colonel: I send forward today by express the list of prisoners of war called for by your telegraphic order of the 4th instant. The number of those who are strictly citizens is comparatively small. The larger share of the list is composed of those whom I have styled bushwhackers. The members of the latter class cannot claim to be prisoners of war, neither can they claim as citizens a trial by the slow and expensive methods of civil law. I would recommend that the most desperate among them be tried by military commissions on the charge of violation of laws and customs of war and that the rest be exchanged.

I have the honor to be, colonel, your obedient servant,

F. A. Dick
Lieutenant-Colonel and Provost-Marshal-General.

Post, Waynesville, Mo., May 15, 1863.

Brig. Gen. Thomas A. Davies
Commanding District of Rolla, Mo.

General: I have just received the important information, from B. Colwin, one of General Herron's scouts, they discovered a large camp of upward of 100 bushwhackers, with a great many stolen horses, in the vicinity of Mountain Store, near Hutton Valley, about 80 miles from this place. I intended to telegraph immediately to the commanding officer at Lebanon, and request him to send about 30 men, under command of Lieutenant David Hunter, who knows that country well, to join my men; but B. Colwin believes that it would be better to postpone an expedition some eight days, in order to lay some traps for them. He will start again on Monday to get all the information he possibly can, and will notify us where our forces, who will be sent after the bushwhackers, can meet him. But I beg to state to you that we have not men enough at this place to send out strong scouting parties, escort the stage and trains, and hold this post; therefore I would suggest to you, if you would send some infantry to hold the post for a short time, our cavalry would be more effective. Infantry would answer all the purpose, especially as forage is scarce in this country; and if you could not send us any from Rolla, would you permit me to call in some of the Enrolled Missouri Militia in this vicinity, to serve at this post on guard duty, when our men have left?

To deceive the people around here, in order to prevent the bushwhackers getting any information, I have circulated the false report that we would be removed from here in some eight or ten days, and some infantry be put in our place.

I am earnestly determined to break up these camps of bushwhackers and marauders, who have recently committed so much depredation, and I hope you will excuse me if I put you to any trouble, and would respectfully request you to give me your assistance and instructions.

Very respectfully, sir, your obedient servant
Waldema Fischer,
Major Fifth Missouri State Militia Cavalry,
Commanding Post

Pilot Knob, Mo., July 27, 1863.

Major-General Schofield

I am advised from Fredericktown that a company of cavalry left by General Davidson at Hog-Eye, Wayne County, guarding subsistence stores, were attacked by guerrillas under Sam Hilderbrand on Saturday night, the 25th instant. Our forces burned the stores and retreated to Cape Girardeau. Colonel Rogers telegraphs me that he thinks it is a big scare. He may look for a pretty big, strong force of raiders from the Pitman's Ferry and Pocahontas route after General Davidson passes through Greene County, Arkansas. The general left Gainesville on the morning of the 23rd instant.

Clinton B. Fisk,
Brigadier-General

Cape Girardeau, Mo., Sept. 25, 1863.

General Fisk, Commanding:

At Chester, Ills. yesterday, I saw powder landed. The amount sold into Missouri from that place is enormous. A very reliable Union man there told me that powder was sold there to go as low down as opposite Memphis. I am fully convinced that it is sold to our swamp guerrillas, such as Sam Hilderbrand, by the keg. One Jew named Black has sold a large quantity to come to this side. I propose that Capt. C. C. Williams, late in the service, now owner of the ferry-boat at that place, be appointed to regulate the trade in contraband of war with Missouri at that place. He is a reliable Union man. He will attend to it for $50 a month. Failing to get him appointed, I shall be compelled to send troops opposite there, and close the trade. The attention of the authorities at Saint Louis has frequently been called to this with no effect. It has been made a regular depot of supplies for guerrillas.

J. B. Rogers,
Colonel, Commanding.

Headquarters,
Glasgow, Mo., September 26, 1863

Colonel Douglass, Mexico:

I returned from a two days' scout below here last night. We ousted Bill Jackson and his gang of thieves, mortally wounded one of them, and, from signs, others, captured 3 horses, 1 Sharps rifle, 1 double-barreled shotgun, 1 Navy revolver, blankets, ammunition, etc. There are three distinct bands in this county, below here, and if I had a few more men I could soon run them out.

John Tillman,
Captain, Commanding Post.

Headquarters District of Southeastern Missouri
Pilot Knob, Mo., November 25, 1863.

Captain Rice:

Hildebrandt, with 20 men, plundered Farmington this afternoon, and left with their pillage on the Jackson road about 4 o'clock. I think you can certainly catch him. Strike swiftly. Keep George W. Hummel. Get horses for his men, and don't stop until you kill these rascals. Go at once. Kill them as you find them.

Clinton B. Fisk,
Brigadier-General.

Headquarters District of Southeastern Missouri,
Pilot Knob, Mo., November 25, 1863.

Captain Rice, Fredericktown:

Hildebrandt must have passed very near your post, as he moved up to Farmington. The people must have known he was in the country. Press every man, horse, and gun you can find, and let the hunt, pursuit, and extermination be sure and swift. A portion of his gang are in Federal uniform.

Clinton B. Fisk,
Brigadier-General.

Patterson, Mo., April 4, 1865.

Colonel Hynes:

I have sent a force to Indian Ford. They will get there by 6 a.m. tomorrow. I will keep a good watch on all the roads that I think the guerrillas are likely to travel. I have no news concerning them.

James Smith,
Captain, Commanding Post.

Warrensburg, Mo., April 5, 1865.

Commanding Office
Lexington, Mo.:

A squad of seven bushwhackers passed Clinton, Henry Co., Mo., yesterday afternoon, going in the direction of Kingsville. They have probably gone into Greenton Valley. I have telegraphed these facts to Pleasant Hill, directing they be followed if possible. If at all practicable you will send after them also.

M. C. Henslee
Major, Commanding Seventh Cavalry Missouri State Militia.

Knobnoster, April 5, 1865.

Captain Laurant:

Mr. J. C. Wingfield, living nine miles south of this place, has just come in here. Reports seven bushwhackers came to his house about daylight, but he was well armed and would not admit them. About 10 a.m. they were at George Peak's house, about a mile east of his house, and was stopping there at the latest account. He refers you to W. E. Chester, of Captain Box's company, for his reliability.

U.S. Military Telegraph Operator.

Weston, April 5, 1865.

Brigadier-General Penick:

Sir: Tinsley was found dead by some people who had been to church in the Boydson neighborhood. Who killed him is not known. He is supposed to have been in company of King Litton and Morton Dryden, two notorious bushwhackers. Particulars tomorrow.

Respectfully, A. G. Beller.

Patterson, Mo., April 25, 1865.

Lieut. Col. F. M. Malone
Pilot Knob, Mo.:

Look out for guerrillas; 200 rebels have just been reported. They were this morning fourteen miles from this post on Bear Creek, marching in the direction of Farmington. I have sent a force to look after them.

James Smith,
Captain, Commanding Post.

Cape Girardeau, Mo., April 25, 1865.

Lieut. P. McRae
Fredericktown:

Keep a sharp lookout for the 200 guerrillas. Call in all the armed citizens.

John L. Beveridge,
Brevet Brigadier-General.

Pilot Knob, Mo., April 25, 1865.

Lieut. Philip McRae

Commanding Post of Fredericktown:

Two hundred guerrillas are coming up toward you from below. Be on your guard. They were on Bear Creek, fourteen miles from Patterson, this morning.

F. M. Malone
Lieutenant-Colonel.

Headquarters Department of the Missouri,
St. Louis, Mo., April 25, 1865.

Col. Chester Harding, Jr.

Comdg. District of Central Missouri, Warrensburg, Mo.:

Colonel: Troops are posted to prohibit guerrillas from crossing the Missouri River, to break up bands of guerrillas near place posted. The troops must be kept under strict discipline, and any depredations upon citizen or property will be severly dealth with. They must confine their duty to military matters and not interfere in civil matters. It will also be their duty to carry out the orders in relation to ferries, which will be furnished them.

I have the honor to be, colonel, your obedient servant,

G. M. Dodge
Major-General, Commanding.

California, Mo. April 25, 1865.

Col. Chester Harding:

Sir: My scouts have returned. No bushwhackers in this vicinity. Forty men, supposed to be rebels, passed north on Sunday. Can I follow up? I respectfully request to be allowed to work my way slowly northward. Please answer.

J. M. Bernard,
Captain.

De Soto, Mo., April 26, 1865.

Major Hannahs,

Acting Assistant Adjutant-General:

Hilderbrand was day before yesterday again four miles east of Big River Mills with some men. It is a new moon again, and he is getting ready for another raid. For pity's sake do detail ten men to Cadet. There are here at De Soto yet thirty-five men for duty, and twenty-five are certainly enough to hold this place. There will be trouble within the next two weeks. Please answer.

F. Kellermann.

St. Louis, April 26, 1865.

General Beveridge
Cape Girardeau:

It is reported that Hilderbrand was four miles east of Big River Mills on the 24th instant.

By order of Brigadier-General Wagner.

H. Hannahs
Major and Acting Assistant Adjutant-General.

Fort Scott, May 9, 1865.

General R. B. Mitchell
Fort Leavenworth:

Henry Taylor's command of bushwhackers with Jesse James and others have broken up into small squads and scattered. The balance have all gone north. They crossed the Osage River near Papinsville, Mo., and Grand River near the east line of Bates County, Mo. My troops followed their trail that far. They claimed to be Shelby's men and committed but few depredations, seeming to be anxious to get through the country as quietly as possible.

C. W. Blair,
Colonel.

Macon, Mo., May 10, 1865.

Maj. J. W. Barnes
Assistant Adjutant-General:

It is reported at these headquarters that three men of the Warren and Montgomery County companies were killed yesterday morning by a gang of twelve bushwhackers between Danville and Portland. The guerrillas were dressed in complete Federal uniform and were taken by the militia for Federal troops. They traveled a mile or two in company, when at a signal from the guerrillas commenced firing. There were 6 militiamen — 3 known to be killed, 2 missing, and 1 escaped. I have 75 men of the Ninth Cavalry Missouri State Militia in pursuit.

W. T. Clarke,
Assistant Adjutant-General

Macon, May 17, 1865

Maj. J. W. Barnes,
Assistant Adjutant-General, St. Louis, Mo.:

Harry Truman is here, representing himself as a scout operating under the orders of General Dodge and the provost-marshal-general. He asks for twenty men and a commissioned officer to aid him in carrying out his plans. Has he any authority for so doing?

A. J. Harding,
Lieutenant, Aide-de-Camp, and
Acting Assistant Adjutant-General.

Macon, May 17, 1865.

Col. J. H. Baker,
Provost-Marshal-General, St. Louis, Mo.:

Harry Truman says he has an arrangement made with the various bands of guerrillas in North Missouri by which they all propose to surrender if they can be released on taking the oath of allegiance. He desires an officer and twenty men to aid in carrying out his scheme. Is he working under orders from you? He asserts that he is.

A. J. Harding,
Lieutenant, Aide-de-Camp, and
Acting Assistant Adjutant-General.

Macon, May 18, 1865.

Maj. J. W. Barnes
Assistant Adjutant-General:

Harry Truman wants an escort of twenty mounted men to go with him to Chariton County to carry out his plan. Shall they be furnished?

A. J. Harding,
Lieutenant and Aide-de-Camp.

Headquarters Department of the Missouri
May 18, 1865.

Lieut. A. J. Harding,
Aide-de-Camp, Macon:

I know nothing about Truman's plans, and no troops will be sent with him until I do.

G. M. Dodge,
Major-General.

Headquarters District of Southwest Missouri,
May 18, 1865.

Lieut. A. J. Harding,
Aide-de-Camp, Macon:

I know nothing about Truman's plans, and no troops will be sent with him until I do.

G. M. Dodge,
Major-General.

Headquarters District of Southwest Missouri,
Springfield, Mo., May 23, 1865.

Maj. J. M. Moore
Commanding at Cassville:

It is probable that a gang of guerrillas, about thirty-five in number, will cross the road going south tonight or tomorrow. This is a most bloody band and will probably pass between Cassville and this place. Do all you can to capture and destroy them. Notify all citizens to be on the lookout. They have killed all citizens who have fallen into their hands, some twenty in all.

John B. Sandborn,
Brevet Major-General, Commanding.

Cape Girardeau, Mo., May 29, 1865.

Major Hannahs,
Acting Assistant Adjutant-General:

Captain Minor reports from Perryville that on the 22nd his company had a fight with the Hilderbrand's gang near Big River Mills. Killed one man and wounded two others. It is supposed that Hilderbrand is dead, as he was one of the wounded.

F. M. Malone,
Lieutenant-Colonel, Commanding.

BIBLIOGRAPHY

American Guide Series, Missouri, Show Me State, Writers' Program, Duell, Sloan & Pearce, N.Y., 1941.

Clarke, Donald Henderson, *Autobiography of Frank Tarbeaux,* Vanguard Press, New York, 1930.

Connelley, William Elsey, *Quantrill and the Border Wars,* Torch Press, Cedar Rapids, Iowa, 1909.

Edwards, John Newman, *Noted Guerrillas,* J. W. Marsh Co., St. Louis, Mo., 1880.

Edwards, John Newman, *Shelby and His Men,* Hudson-Kimberly Publishers, Kansas City, Mo., 1897.

Breihan, Carl W., *Quantrill and His Guerrillas,* Swallow Press, Denver, Colorado, 1959.

Breihan, Carl W., *Killer Legions of Quantrill,* Superior Publishing Co., Seattle, Washington, 1971

Buel, James William, *The Border Outlaws,* Historical Publishing Co., St. Louis, Mo., 1881.

Forest, Col. Cris, *Hildebrand, the Outlaw,* Robert DeWitt Publishers, New York, 1869.

Thompson, Henry C., *Sam Hildebrand Rides Again,* Steinbeck Publishing Co., Bonne Terre, Mo., 1950.

Triplett, Frank, *Life, Times, and Death of Jesse James,* J. H. Chambers & Co., St. Louis, Mo., 1882.

OTHER SOURCES

DuQuoin, Illinois, Tribune, Issues of March 28, April 4, April 11, and April 18, 1872.

Missouri Republican, Issues of April 1st through April 17th, 1872.

St. Louis Globe Democrat, Issues of April, 1872.

Histories of Jefferson County, Washington County, Perry County, Ste. Genevieve, St. François, Cape Girardeau Counties, and Iron,

Butler, and Ripley Counties, in Missouri.
Personal contact with Edward McArtor, whose father fought with Sam Hildebrand, and who graciously allowed me the use of his father's diary and papers.
War of the Rebellion, Compilation of Official Records, Union and Confederate Armies. Washington, Government Printing Office, 1899.
Personal notes of L. J. Hildebrand, nephew of Sam Hildebrand.